THE BOOK
OF
IQ Tests

THE BOOK
OF
IQ Tests

by Philip J. Carter
& Kenneth A. Russell

STERLING
New York

STERLING
New York

An Imprint of Sterling Publishing
387 Park Avenue South
New York, NY 10016

Published in 2007 by Sterling Publishing Co., Inc.
© 2000 by Philip J. Carter and Kenneth A. Russell
Designed by StarGraphics Studio

ISBN 978-1-4027-5735-8

Library of Congress Cataloging-in-Publication Data Available

Distributed in Canada by Sterling Publishing
c/o Canadian Manda Group, 165 Dufferin Street
Toronto, Ontario, Canada M6K 3H6
Distributed in the United Kingdom by GMC Distribution Services
Castle Place, 166 High Street, Lewes, East Sussex, England BN7 1XU
Distributed in Australia by Capricorn Link (Australia) Pty. Ltd.
P.O. Box 704, Windsor, NSW 2756, Australia

For information about custom editions, special sales, and premium and corporate purchases,
please contact Sterling Special Sales at 800-805-5489 or specialsales@sterlingpublishing.com.

Manufactured in China

20 19 18 17 16 15 14 13 12 11

www.sterlingpublishing.com

CONTENTS

INTRODUCTION

Intelligence is the ability to adapt to new situations, think abstractly, and comprehend complex ideas. IQ is the abbreviation for Intelligence Quotient. The word "quotient" means the results of dividing one quantity by another.

An intelligence test (IQ Test) is a standardized test designed to measure human intelligence as distinct from attainments. The aim of the twenty-five tests in this book is to give your brain a thorough mental workout and to familiarize yourself with the various types of questions you are likely to encounter when taking a supervised test.

The questions are challenging, and deliberately so, as this is the only way to boost your performance and increase your brainpower.

But above all, the tests are designed to entertain. It is, therefore, up to you as to how you wish to use the book—either to test yourself or your friends on each test against the clock, or simply to dip into the book at random and attempt whichever of the one thousand questions that takes your fancy at the time.

It's your choice, but whichever way you choose to use the book, have fun, enjoy the questions, and happy solving!

For readers wishing to assess their performance, a time limit of 90 minutes is allowed for each test.

Use the following scoring table for each test:

Score	Rating
36-40	Exceptional
31-35	Excellent
25-30	Very Good
19-20	Good
14-18	Average

TEST 1

1. Read clockwise to figure out this sixteen-letter word. Only alternate letters are shown, and you have to find the starting point.

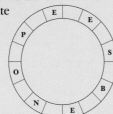

2. What number should replace the question mark?

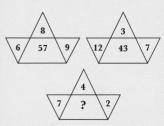

3. Only one set of letters to the right can be arranged into a five-letter English word. Can you find the word?

BYRDI	TONET	NRCOL
PUITN	HUTME	LEBIT
TINOL	RUGNE	BEHAD

4.

as

is to:

A   B   C   D

5. Which three-letter word forms two other words that are unrelated in meaning when "LESS" and "NESS" are added to the end? For example, SOUND: SOUNDLESS, SOUNDNESS.
Clue: *Foolish deponent*

6. Which number is the odd one out?

563 572
671 594 916
945 832 298
635 829 752
176 196 294
283

7. I create a happy sound on my entire journey to a place of monetary deposit. What am I doing?

8. Which word comes closest in meaning to METE?

CARRY, ADJOIN, COORDINATE, ALLOT, PARODY

9. Only ten letters of the alphabet do not appear in this grid. What ten-letter phrase can they be arranged to spell out?
Clue: *Cape Canaveral*

P	Z	B	G
M	O	K	J
F	W	Q	X
Y	V	R	D

10. What number comes next in this sequence?

483, 759, 264, 837, ?

11. What symbol should replace the question mark?

12. One letter in each word of a well-known saying has been changed. What is the saying?

TAPE TIE PULL MY TOE CORNS

13. What, in connection with this question, is the next number below?

4, 13, 19, 21, 29, ?

14. To what number should the missing hand on the clock point?

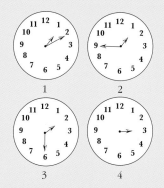

1   2

3   4

15. Fill in the blanks with the same seven letters in the same order so that the sentence makes complete sense.

A _____ chef was _____ to serve the meal because he had _____.

16. LEA : PIE
SAP :

(a) BAT   (d) WET
(b) WAG   (e) YET
(c) BOW

17. What phrase is suggested at right?

SH
TT
RG
EN

18. What number should appear in the circle with the question mark?

19. What face should replace the question mark?

A   B   C   D   E

20. Fill in the missing word to complete the crossword.

21.

is to ╲ as ╱ is to:

A   B   C   D

22. EUPHORIA is to BLISS as MELANCHOLY is to:

(a) BAWDY   (c) DESPAIR
(b) UNSEEMLY   (d) NEGATE
(e) RIBALD

23. Place two of the four-letter groups together to make a word.

RIAL - SYCO - TUTO - PANT - PLAT

24. Which pentagon continues the series?

A   B   C

25. Find a one-word anagram in CREAM ELK.

26. Simplify $\dfrac{5}{11} \div \dfrac{25}{22}$.

27. Trace out a ten-letter word in any direction, using each letter once only.

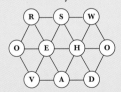

28. Simplify $\dfrac{725}{1000}$ as a fraction.

29. Which word means the fear of MICE?

    (a) ANEMOPHOBIA
    (b) MUSOPHOBIA
    (c) BAROPHOBIA
    (d) POTOPHOBIA
    (e) OCHOPHOBIA

30. What is the meaning of PRANDIAL?

    (a) BREAKFAST
    (b) TEATIME
    (c) DINNER
    (d) SUPPER
    (e) SNACKS

31. A word can be placed inside the parentheses that has the same meaning as the words outside. What is it?

    TAR (_ _ _ _ _) SET UP

32. If $4 \times 4 = 20$, then $5 \times 6 = $?

33. Which circle's letters cannot be rearranged into a six-letter word?

  A   B   C   D

34. Which number should replace the question mark?

6	8	17	21
13	1	9	10
3	15	4	?
4	6	4	5

35. What is the opposite of NEOPHYTE?

    (a) EARTHLY   (d) EXPERT
    (b) NOVICE   (e) STARLIKE
    (c) ANCIENT

36. What number should replace the question mark?

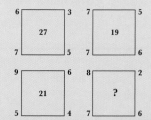

37. Which animal does not fit with the others?

(a) CHAMOIS   (d) FENNEC
(b) TIERCEL   (e) GERBIL
(c) IMPALA   (f) JERBOA

38. Place the letters in the grid to make a flower and a fish.

G O P P P P U Y Y

39. What is the mathematical sign for "identical with"?

(a)   [ ]
(b)   >
(c)   ≡
(d)   /
(e)   <

40. Complete the word.

_ _ C K J _ _

TEST 2

1. Change SEPTEMBER to JULY. The asterisks in each word are common to the word above it.

SEPTEMBER

Clue: *Hygenic*
Clue: *Anthropod*
Clue: *Numerous*

JULY

2. What number should replace the question mark?

2	9	7
10	?	12
8	13	5

3. The following clue leads to what pair of rhyming words?

SKILLFUL ROBBERY

4. Add one letter, not necessarily the same letter, to each word to find eight words that all have something in common.

MAT, SEW, ART, SAG, BAN, FAN, ICE

8. What well-known proverb is opposite in meaning to the proverb "Too many cooks spoil the broth"?

5. Which day is two days before the day after the day three days after the day before Tuesday?

SUNDAY
MONDAY
TUESDAY
WEDNESDAY
THURSDAY
FRIDAY
SATURDAY

9. How many lines appear below?

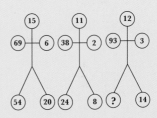

6. Which of the numbered figures is the odd one out?

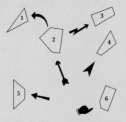

10. What number should replace the question mark?

7. A pancake can be sliced into four pieces in any number of ways by using two cuts. One example is shown to the right. What is the maximum number of pieces that can be obtained from a pancake using three cuts?

11. All widgets are green. Everything green has a hole in the middle. Some things that are green have a jagged edge. Therefore:

1. All widgets have a hole in the middle.
2. Everything with a jagged edge is a widget.
3. Neither of the above is true.
4. Both the above are true.

12. What number should replace the question mark?

13. Unscramble these four anagrammed words to determine what they have in common.

OGLED, WROTE, CLEATS, PELMET

14. Which is the odd one out?

A   B   C   D

15. What number should replace the question mark?

16. Rearrange the two five-letter words to form a ten-letter word meaning "trader with Native Americans."

MOOCH CANER

17. Which word means the same as VIBRATO?

(a) LUSTROUS
(b) EXCITING
(c) THROBBING
(d) SOFTLY
(e) STATIONARY

18. Insert the letters of the phrase FAMILIES MASS SALE into the empty spaces below, using each letter once to complete a palindromic sentence—one that reads the same backwards and forwards. For example: MADAM, I'M ADAM.

_A _ _ _ _ _ _ S _ _ _ _ _ _ _ _ _ S _ _ _ _

Clue: *Relatively altruistic*

19. "The chance of exposure to the adverse consequences of future events." Which word fits closest to the above definition?

(a) SPECULATION
(b) DANGER
(c) RISK
(d) WORRY
(e) HALLUCINATION

20. What number continues this sequence?

8960, 6720, 3360, 840, 630, ?

21. What number should replace the question mark?

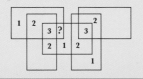

22. Which two words below are closest in meaning?

AUTHENTIC, GERMANE, FOREIGN, GENTLE, PRODIGIOUS, COGNATE

23. Place three of the two-letter groups together to form a fruit.

OR – LY – AN – EE – GO – CH

24. Which is the missing square?

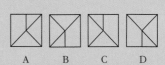

A   B   C   D

25. Which word will fit in front of these words to make new words?

(_ _ _ _)

BOOT
POT
ASS
DAW
HAMMER

29. What is the surface area of this tennis ball?

2½ in.

(a) 17.635 sq. in.
(b) 18.635 sq. in.
(c) 19.635 sq. in.
(d) 20.635 sq. in.
(e) 21.635 sq. in.

26. There is a system for pricing the menu. What would oysters cost?

MENU	
SOUP	$18
SALAD	$23
ROAST BEEF	$41
ICE CREAM	$36
COFFEE	$27

30. Which of the following is always associated with HAMSTRING?

(a) PIGS
(b) BACON
(c) TENNIS RACQUETS
(d) DINNER
(e) TENDON

27. Which number should replace the question mark?

28. If the missing letters in the circle at right, are correctly inserted, they will form an eight-letter word. The word will not have to be read in a clockwise direction, but the letters are consecutive. What is the word and missing letters?

31. What number should replace the question mark?

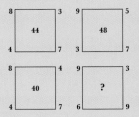

32. What number should replace the question mark?

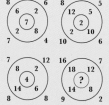

33. The vowels have been omitted from this quotation. Can you replace them?

T S W S F T H R T H T K
N W S H S W N C H L D

34. Place the letters in the grid to form a nautical person and a mineral.

A A C
E F I P
L O R
R R D

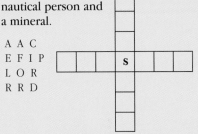
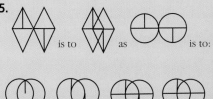

35.

is to   as   is to:

A   B   C   D

36. Which of the boxes below is most like the box on the right?

A   B   C   D

37. Fill in the missing letters to make a nine-letter word starting from a corner square and spiraling into the center.

U		E
	E	R
E	T	A

38. What number should replace the question mark?

7 11 20 ? 61 97 146

39. By moving through the doorways, spell out an eight-letter word. Each letter may be used only once.

40. Fill in the missing letters to make a nine-letter word starting from a corner square and continuing in a spiral to the center.

O		E
W	S	R
O	L	

TEST 3

1. Complete the word below that contains a unique trigraph—i.e., three consecutive letters which appear in no other English word.

_ _ _ _ KSG _ _ _ _ _

2. Find just one reason for arranging the following words into three groups, each containing three words:

MONKEY, LOANED, CORNER, LONGER, BLONDE, SPONGE, HORNET, WONDER, BRONZE

3. By joining corners and not counting rotations and reflections it is possible to dissect a pentagon into three triangles only one way and a hexagon three different ways. Both are illustrated below:

In how many ways is it possible to dissect a heptagon into triangles?

4. What completes the below sequence?

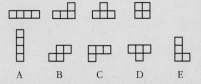

A   B   C   D   E

5. LARGO : SLOW
PIANO :

A.   SMOOTH
B.   LOUD
C.   SOFT
D.   PLAY
E.   BRISK

6. What number should replace the question mark?

7. Tom beats Joe at pool but loses to Sue. Hilary usually wins against Joe, sometimes against Tom, but never against Sue. Who is the weakest player?

8. Solve the cryptic clue below. The answer is a ten-letter anagram contained within the clue:

ESCORT A MAN
UNSTEADILY TO
CALIFORNIAN CITY

9. Working clockwise, take one letter from each circle in turn to spell out two synonyms. **Note:** *Each word starts in a different circle.*

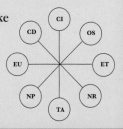

10. The die is rolled one face to Square 2, and so on—one face at a time to Squares 3-4-5-6. Which number will appear on the top face in Square 6?

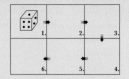

11. Which number is the odd one out?

3628, 2426, 4146, 1448

12. Insert the numbers 1–5 in the circles, using each number once. Do so in such a way that for any particular circle the sum of the number in the circles connected directly to it add up to the value allocated to the number inside the circle in accordance with the table below:

1 = 5
2 = 12
3 = 7
4 = 2
5 = 6

EXAMPLE:

1 = 14 (4 + 7 + 3)
4 = 8 (7 + 1)
7 = 5 (4 + 1)
3 = 1

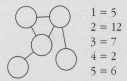

13.

is to   as

is to:

A   B   C

D   E

14. Arrange these words in alphabetical order.

ABOUND   ABSCOND
ABALONE   ABDOMEN
ABDICATE   ABROGATES
ABANDON

15. Insert a word in the parentheses that means the same as the definitions outside the parentheses:

HASTEN (   ) GRASSLIKE PLANT

16. If meat in a river (3 in 6) is T(HAM)ES, can you find a thin rope in an instrument (4 in 9)?

17. Arrange the letters in the squares below to find two nine-letter words that are antonyms.

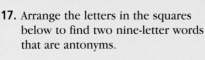

18. What number should replace the question mark?

8   9   7

81   42   ?

4   6   3   12   8   6

19. The words BLACK and WHITE are antonyms. What two words, one rhyming with BLACK and one with WHITE, are also antonyms?

20. Which is the missing square?

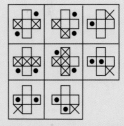

A   B   C   D

21. Find pairs of letters to form four four-letter musical instruments— one pair is not used.

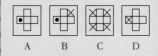

BA	HA	LU
TE	FE	OB
FI	OE	TU

22. What number should replace the question mark?

Simplify: $5 + 8 \div 4 + 9 \times 2 + 7 = ?$

23. Find a six-letter word made up of only the four following letters:

ON
IP

24. Place two of the three-letter groups together to form an article of clothing.

SOC - TER - COA - JER - KIT - SHI - KIN - RTY

25. Which two words are similar in meaning?

PLUNDER, CHARM, JOSH, WEAN, TEASE, CHANGE

26. Which of these is the odd one out?

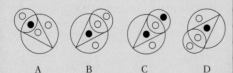

A   B   C   D

27. Which diagram continues the sequence?

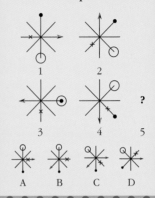

28. Rearrange the letters in each set to form the name of a plant.

29. Find the missing word that will fit the rule of the example below.

CONE (NICK) KRIS
LISP (_ _ _ _) ETON

30. A stone is dropped over the edge of a cliff. After 5 seconds how many feet has it fallen?

(a) 280 ft.
(b) 320 ft.
(c) 400 ft.
(d) 480 ft.
(e) 500 ft.

31. Starting at a corner square, move along a spiral route and find the rule for the numbering to replace the question mark.

32	28	34	30
26	42	38	36
30	36	?	32
24	40	34	38

32. How many revolutions are made by a 28-inch bicycle wheel over 1 mile?

(a) 620
(b) 720
(c) 820
(d) 920
(e) 1020

33. Draw the next figure in this series.

?

34. What is the mathematical sign for infinity?

(a) ∢
(b) ∞
(c) Δ
(d) ∷
(e) ∝

35. Fill in the blanks to find three islands:

_ H _ I _ T _ A _
_ A _ R _ T _ U _
_ A _ K _ A _ D

36. Find a three-letter word that completes all three words on the left-hand side and prefixes all three words on the right-hand side.

HAS   DON
ROT   (_ _ _)   PIN
FAT   ANT

37. On which target have 185 points been scored?

A   B   C   D

38. Which of the following is always part of SAUERKRAUT?

CHEESE, HOT WATER, MILK, BUTTER, CABBAGE

39. Place a word in the parentheses that when placed at the end of the first word makes a word and when placed in front of the second word also makes a word.

QUARTER (_ _ _ _) HAND

40.

 is to as

K L M is to:

A   B   C   D

TEST 4

1. Which is the odd one out?

A   B   C   D   E   F   G   H   I   J   K   L

2. Solve the anagram in parentheses to correctly complete the quotation.

Failure is the only opportunity to begin again, more (leniently gilt).
—*Henry Ford*

3. Pair the eight words below to form four hyphenated words. Use each word once only.

GROUP, STILL, TYPING, AGE, STOCK, SIZE, BLOOD, TWIN

4. Mitzi has $800 to spend. She spends $\frac{2}{5}$ of the $800 on clothes, 0.425 of the $800 on jewelry, and writes out a check for $240 for a new watch. What is her financial situation at the end of the day?

5. Which word is opposite in meaning to OPTIMUM?

ANTITHESIS, UNORIGINAL, LEAST, STARK, CHASTE

6. What is the missing number?

5	3	8	4	9	6	8
8	6	6	1	8	4	?
3	2	7	6	8	7	3

7. GAZEBO
ACCEDE
VERIFY

Which girl's name continues the above sequence?

A. EUNICE   C. JOANNE
B. AGATHA   D. INGRID

8. Solve the two anagrams to produce a well-known saying.

_ _ _   _ _ _   _ _ _   _ _ _   _ _   _ _ _   _ _ _

THE CATTLE   HATE BUT GOOF

9. When the shape below is folded to form a cube, just one of the following can be produced. Which one?

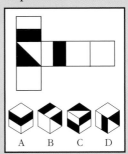

10. If 9L of a C is 9 lives of a cat, can you decode the following?

10P in C

11. Solve the clues to find four six-letter words. The same three letters are represented by XYZ in each word.

X	Y	Z	_	_	_	**Clue:** *Fleet*
_	X	Y	Z	_	_	**Clue:** *Heat*
_	_	X	Y	Z	_	**Clue:** *Beguiles*
_	_	_	X	Y	Z	**Clue:** *Remove defensive capability*

12. What number should replace the question mark?

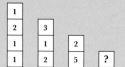

14. Spiral clockwise to find a ten-letter word. You must find the starting point and provide the missing letters. The word you are looking for starts and finishes with the same two letters.

13. The word SOLO appears only once in this grid in a straight line. Can you find it? It may appear horizontally, vertically or diagonally, backwards or forwards.

S	O	L	S	L	O	S	O
S	O	S	O	S	O	O	S
O	O	S	O	S	L	O	O
O	S	O	L	S	O	O	O
S	O	S	L	S	L	L	O
L	S	L	O	O	S	O	S
O	O	O	S	S	O	O	L
O	S	L	L	O	S	L	O

15. Which is the odd one out?

16. We all have the _____1_____ to put our _____2_____ to even more use by _____3_____ new avenues, experiences, and _____4_____ adventures.

Select the correct words (one each) from the choices below to correctly complete the above statement.

1. privilege, sense, capacity, preference, imagination
2. computers, money, ability, brain, vitality
3. exploring, finding, arranging, touring, crossing
4. dangerous, modern, subtle, discreet, learned

17. Insert a girl's name into the bottom line and complete the three-letter words.

H	C	F	F	A	E	S	T
I	U	U	O	L	G	I	I

18. What number should replace the question mark?

37 95 22
58 106 21
96 ? 23

20. What well-known phrase is indicated to the right?

```
C O B   L T
C O   A L T
C   B A L T
C O B A   T
C O B A L
```

19. DYNAMIC (ADORN) PROFUSE

Using the same rules as the example above, what word should appear in the parentheses below?

RETORTS (_ _ _ _ _) LIBERTY

21. What is the total of the numbers on the reverse of these dice?

22. Which of these is the odd one out?

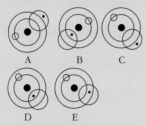

A B C

D E

23. Which of these is not an anagram of currency?

(a) ZETQULEA   (b) YOMASED
(c) DASRUCO   (d) VILBAOR
(e) TATRES   (f) TERECSES

24. Find a one-word anagram in:

SORE CAT

25. Place four of the three-letter groups together to make two six-letter words.

SUT - TIC - NAU - TIN - HER - MET - SEA - MIT

26. Fill in the blank spaces to spell out three dances.

_ I _ T _ R _ U _
_ U _ D _ I _ L _
_ O _ O _ A _ S _

27. Which two words have opposite meanings?

LADYLIKE, SUCCINCT,
TURBULENT, COMMODIOUS,
HOYDENISH, EMACIATED

28. If the missing letters in the two circles to the right are correctly inserted they will form synonyms. The words do not have to be read in a clock-wise direction, but the letters are consecutive. What are the words and missing letters?

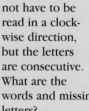

29. LING is to FISH as CARAVEL is to:

(a) MINSTREL
(b) CARAVAN
(c) CIRCUS
(d) VEHICLE
(e) BOAT

30. What roman numeral should replace the question mark?

31. What number should replace the question mark?

7   17 $8\frac{1}{2}$ $14\frac{1}{4}$ 10 $11\frac{1}{2}$?

32. What is the meaning of MANTILLA?

(a) TROUSERS
(b) SHIP
(c) DRESS
(d) LOGANBERRIES
(e) SCARF

33. There are only five regular solids with symmetrical faces. Which one of these has twenty faces?

(a) ICOSAHEDRON
(b) DODECAHEDRON
(c) CUBE
(d) TETRAHEDRON
(e) OCTAHEDRON

34. How many degrees is this angle?

(a) 105°
(b) 110°
(c) 115°
(d) 120°
(e) 130°

35. What is x?

$$\frac{4 \times 2 - 6}{7 - 4 \times 2} = x$$

36. HIPPOPHOBIA is to HORSES as AILUROPHOBIA is to:

(a) ELEPHANTS
(b) LIONS
(c) MICE
(d) SHARKS
(e) CATS

37. Which word can be placed at the end of these words to make new words?

STIR
KIND
SAC (_ _ _)
BAR
HAT

38. Complete the word.

_ _ U B R _ _ _ _

39. Which circle's letters cannot be rearranged into a six-letter word?

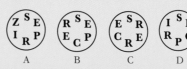

A   B   C   D

40. NECTAR is to DRINK as AMBROSIA is to:

(a) MEDICINE   (b) BEES   (c) GREECE
(d) TONIC   (e) FOOD

TEST 5

1. What word should replace the question mark?

2. What do these words have in common?

AMULET
DEMURE
MORATORIUM
MULTIGERM

3. Consider the following square:

Now consider the following array:

Which square should replace the question mark?

A   B   C   D

4. "An adventurous action that runs counter to approved or conventional conduct." What word fits closest to this definition?

A. MISDEMEANOR
B. ESCAPADE
C. EXPERIENCE
D. VENTURE
E. EXPLORATION

7. Which number is the odd one out?

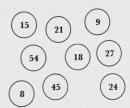

5. Move from star to star to spell out a ten-letter word.

8. Find the starting point and visit each square once to reach the treasure marked T.

1N 2W
= 1 North
2 West

1S 1E	1S 1E	2S
1S	T	1N 2W
1E 2N	2N 1E	2W 1N

N
W — E
S

6. Sam visited several places in Europe.

He hated Madrid.
He loved Prague.
He hated Warsaw.
He hated Antrim.
He loved Ankara.

Did he love or hate Vienna?

9. Which is the odd one out?

ACETATE
NYLON
POLYESTER
VICUNA
RAYON

10. Solve each anagram to find two phrases that are spelled differently but sound alike. For example: A NAME, AN AIM.

IDLE LURES   ROSY DOLL

11. Insert two words that are anagrams of each other to complete the sentence. For example: She removed the <u>stain</u> from her new <u>satin</u> blouse.

Cheated out of what was rightfully mine, it would be a long, hard battle before I could _____ my inheritance. My solicitor warned me I could only hope for a _____, but I was determined to fight to the bitter end.

12. What number is three places away from itself plus 4, two places away from itself minus 3, three places from itself doubled, two places away from itself minus 1, three places from itself plus 3, and two places away from itself minus 5?

19	14	3	8	11
9	2	20	6	5
15	22	16	2	30
24	7	18	4	10
18	1	12	13	17

13. Which shape continues the sequence below?

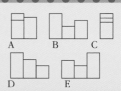

14. Underline the two words in parentheses that the word outside the parentheses always has.

RIVER (ESTUARY, WATER, BOATS, MOVEMENT, WATERFALL)

15. What letter should replace the question mark?

16. Which is the missing section?

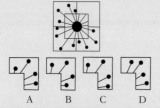

A   B   C   D

17. The cost of hiring a private rail carriage is shared equally by all the passengers. The carriage has seats for forty passengers and the total bill amounts to $70.37. How many passenger seats are not occupied?

18. What word is indicated from the clues below?

The bottom of the heap,
The end of the line,
The first of all,
The center of artichoke,
The beginning of the end.

19. Divide 800 by $\frac{1}{4}$ and add 5. What is the answer?

20. Rearrange the tiles so that every two horizontally adjacent letters form a word, and two related words can be read around the outer edge.

21.

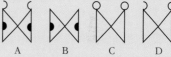

is to ... as ... is to:

A   B   C   D

22. Place the letters in the grid to make a color and a lizard.

AAGHIKKNUI

23. What number comes next in the series?

0.5	(a) 0.857
0.666	(b) 0.861
0.75	(c) 0.865
0.8	(d) 0.869
0.833	(e) 0.873

24. What is the name given to a group of turtles?

(a) TRAIL
(b) SHELL
(c) KNOT
(d) WADDLE
(e) BALE
(f) NEST

25. Place three of the two-letter groups together to form a bird.

AN - IN - PI - DU - GE - NL

26. Simplify: $\dfrac{1}{3} \div \dfrac{7}{18}$

27. Which is the odd one out?

A   B   C

28. There is an odd letter in each hexagon. Can you find them?

1   2   3

29. Which of these is not a bird?

(a) PUFFIN
(b) SISKIN
(c) CALABASH
(d) MALLARD
(e) MERLIN
(f) GOSHAWK

30. Find a twelve-letter bird made up of two six-letter words.

Six letters inside
Six letters outside

31. What symbol should continue the series?

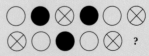

?

32. By moving through the doorways, spell out an eight-letter word.

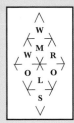

33. Which word means the fear of travel?

(a) HODOPHOBIA
(b) NELOPHOBIA
(c) IDEOPHOBIA
(d) ANDROPHOBIA
(e) HYDROPHOBIA

34. Find three animals hidden in the following sentence:

"In the current times everyone will be a saver at least once with a pension."

35. How many degrees are there in this angle?

(a) 100°   (c) 108°   (e) 120°
(b) 105°   (d) 110°

36. What number should replace the question mark below?

37. Fill in the missing letters to make a nine-letter word, starting from a corner square and continuing in a spiral to the center.

	E	I
I	D	N
A	R	

38. How many different teams of eleven players can be selected from fifteen members?

39. Fill in the missing letter to fit the rule of this pattern.

40. Change this fraction to a decimal.

$$\frac{3}{8} = \text{ ?}$$

TEST 6

1. Complete the grid with the letters MAGIC so that no row, column, or diagonal line contains the same letter more than once.

4. Which is the odd one out?

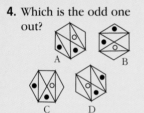

2. I have correctly and accurately made a clear impact with the crown of a small fastener. What have I done?

3. If a car had increased its average speed for a 210-mile journey by 5 mph, the journey would have been completed in 1 hour less. What was the original speed of the car for the journey?

5. What number should replace the question mark?

9	4	6	11
3	6	7	4
5	?	4	1
11	6	3	8

6. Add three consecutive letters of the alphabet to the group of letters below, without splitting the consecutive letters, to form another word.

DY

7. Which word is opposite in meaning to CORPULENT?

OVERWROUGHT, COMMUNAL, HEALTHY, POOR, GAUNT

8. Which one of the following is not an anagram of LITTLE GIANT ENCYCLOPEDIA?

POLITICALLY DECENT EATING
ENTICED PATIENT LOGICALLY
IDENTICALLY ELECTING POET
ALLOCATED NICE TINY PIGLET
TANGENTIALLY CITED POLICE
DETECTING ALIAN OPTICALLY

9. Which month comes next?

JANUARY, MARCH, JUNE, OCTOBER, MARCH, ?

10. What letter should replace the question mark?

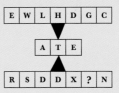

11. Which circles should replace the ones with the question mark?

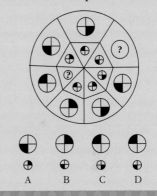

12. What number should replace the question mark in the circle?

13. Seven synonyms of the keyword are shown. Take one letter from each of the seven synonyms in turn to spell out an eighth synonym of the keyword.

Keyword: TALENT
Synonyms: GIFT, ABILITY, KNACK, GENIUS, FLAIR, APTITUDE, CAPACITY

14. Following the rule of the sequence of numbers, what number should come next?

1, 4, 7, 11, 15, 13, 17, ?

15. REAR (LORRAINE) LION
What girl's name should go in the parentheses below according to the same rules as in the example above?

REIN (   ) AGOG

16. Which is the odd one out?

A   B   C   D

17. Four balls are placed in a row. The red ball is next to the green ball but not next to the blue ball. The yellow ball is not next to the blue ball. What ball is next to the yellow ball?

A. The red ball
B. The green ball
C. The red and the green ball
D. There is insufficient information to determine

18. One letter in each word of a well-known saying has been changed. What is the saying?

OLD ORE NUT

19. "An indirect, ingenious, and often cunning means to gain an end."

What word most closely fits the above definition?

PLAN, STRATAGEM, EXPEDIENCY, DIVERSION, FRAUD

20. Taking the respective numerical position of letters in the alphabet, decode the series of numbers in the box.

135144512191915814

For example: LITTLE GIANT = 12920201257911420

L	I	T	T	L	E	G	I	A	N	T
12	9	20	20	12	5	7	9	1	14	20

21. What number comes next in the series?

22. What number should replace the question mark?

	2	
7	4	4

	1	
3	9	8

	4	
6	9	?

23. Find the missing word that will fit the rule of the example below.

ROPE (PART) ANTE
SHAM (_ _ _ _) PIER

24. If $3 \times 6 = 24$,
then $4 \times 3 = ?$

25. What is the missing number?

24	1	4	3
18	1	4	1
30	1	4	?

26. Starting at an outside square and moving in any direction, spell out a ten-letter name of a girl.

EG	NA	MO
AR	LD	RA
DE	BO	HI

27. A word can be placed in the parentheses that has the same meaning as the words outside. What is it? Each dash represents a letter.

STEAL (_ _ _ _ _)
COOK IN WATER

28. The Beaufort wind scale is numbered from 0 to 17. Which number denotes a storm?

(a) 8   (d) 11
(b) 9   (e) 12
(c) 10

29. Trace out a ten-letter word in any direction, using each letter once only.

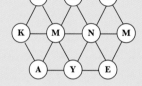

30. Place four of the three-letter groups together to make two six-letter words.

TTI - VIS - CAN - DER - ODI - MUR - OUS - SEC

31. What is the mathematical sign for arc of a circle?

(a) →   (c) ∪   (e) ▭

(b) ●   (d) ⌒

32. What number should replace the question mark?

1   12 $3\frac{1}{4}$ $10\frac{1}{2}$ $5\frac{1}{2}$ 9 $7\frac{3}{4}$?

33. Complete the word. _ _ _ G H C _ _ _

34. Simplify $\frac{675}{1000}$ as a fraction.

35. Fill in the blanks to find four girls' names.

A		N		E
E				I
E		I		A

36. Find the complete word that contains these middle letters. The word is hyphenated.

Z Z Y W

37. Fill in the spaces to spell out three occupations.

_ I _ N _ L _ A _
_ O _ D _ L _ E _
_ A _ N _ Q _ I _

38. Complete the sequence.

39. Which word will fit in front of these words to make new words?

(_ _ _)

HEAD
PRICK
STRIPE
BALL
CUSHION

40. With a standard six-sided die, how many throws are required on average before each of the six numbers has landed faceup?

(a) 10   (b) 15   (c) 20   (d) 25

TEST 7

1. Which four of the five pieces below can be used to construct a perfect circle?

2. Which two of the following words are closest in meaning?

EXOTERIC, RECONDITE, PLAIN, DARK, REASONABLE, ROSEATE

3. Arrange the letters in the squares to find two nine-letter words that are antonyms.

	U	R	P
V	D	R	T	O
S	R	E	S	P
Y	A	A		

4. In which of the sentences below does the name of an animal *not* appear?

A. I was suddenly confronted by a group of evil-doers and hardened criminals.

B. Their leader appeared to be a swarthy, well-dressed Latin American wearing thick-rimmed, tinted spectacles.

C. "Who is this?" said a small, squat individual. "I don't trust him; he could be armed."

D. The leader roared with laughter and gesticulated with his bejewelled arm. "Believe me, he is quite harmless," he said, "but escort him from the premises immediately."

E. I walked out into the cold night air with a huge sigh of relief. This time I had avoided the trap easily, but I knew I might not be so lucky next time.

5. What number should replace the question mark?

6. What letter is immediately to the left of the letter two to the right of the letter four to the left of the letter two to the right of the letter C?

7. Which is the odd one out?

REAMER, GIMLET, CLEAVER, WIMBLE, AUGER

8. Which numbers should replace the question marks?

78	64	62	48	46	32
79	67	63	51	47	35
76	?	?	50	44	34
74	?	?	52	42	36
75	71	59	55	43	39
72	70	56	54	40	38

66	61
69	58

66	61
68	56

66	60
68	58

64	61
69	56

A   B   C   D

9. Place two of the three-letter groups together to form a food.

POT - MEL - CAR - SLI - OAT - WHE - MUE - ATE

10. What do the following words have in common?

APPROPRIATE
BOW
DESERT
DOVE
ENTRANCE
GILL
LEAD
SLAVER

11. You have a range of weights available from 1 to 10. They are all single weights. Which one should you use to balance the 10 ft. scale, and where should you place it?

12.

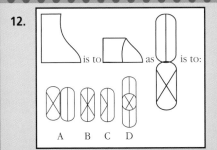

13.

20 / 18 is to 36 / 15 as

72 / 51 is to:

36 / 24	68 / 24	68 / 36	36 / 68
A	B	C	D

14. Think of a four-letter word that reverses its meaning when the letter "T" is placed in front of it.

15. What letter should replace the question mark?

16. The following is extracted from what hyphenated word?

_ _ _ _ S – EX _ _ _ _ _ _ _ _ _

Clue: *Third degree*

---

17. SHORT LANCE is an anagram of which American city?

---

18. In a game of six players that lasts for 50 minutes, two reserves substitute for each player so that all players, including reserves, are on the field for the same length of time. How long is each player on the field?

---

19. What comes next in the below sequence?

A   B   C   D

---

20. OVERUSED : CLICHÉD
OVERATTENTIVE :

CHINTZY, SCHOLASTIC, IRRITABLE, IMPERIOUS, OFFICIOUS

---

21. What is the meaning of TULLE?

(A) VEGETABLE   (D) TENSILE
(B) SILK FABRIC   (E) WEAPON
(C) A MYSTIC

---

22. Fill in the blanks to find three minerals.

_ L _ M _ N _ M
_ A _ N _ S _ U _
_ A _ G _ N _ S _

---

23. Find a one-word anagram from the two words below.

DEEP DRESS

---

24. Which word continues this sequence?

SON, EAT, WORTH, ?

(A) REEL   (C) DEATH
(B) LUNG   (D) PINE

25. Which arrangement of pipes would carry most water?

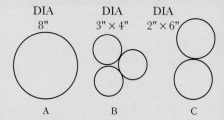

DIA 8"

DIA 3" × 4"

DIA 2" × 6"

A   B   C

26. Which are the odd ones out?

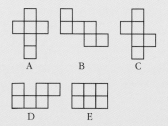

A   B   C

D   E

27. Which of the following metals is always associated with GALVANIZING?

(A) COPPER

(B) BRONZE

(C) ZINC

(D) LEAD

(E) SILVER

28. By moving through the doorways spell out an eight-letter word.

29. Make one word using all ten letters.

TRIBE COSTS

Clue: *Pertaining to midwifery*

30. If the missing letters in the circle are correctly inserted they will form an eight-letter word. The word will not have to be read in a clock-wise direction, but the letters are consecutive. What is the word and missing letters?

31. What number will replace the question mark?

28   47   85   ?   218   313   427

---

32. A well-known phrase has had all its vowels removed and has been split into groups of three letters. What is the phrase? All remaining letters are in the correct order.

HRT DYG NTM RRW

---

33. What number should replace the question mark?

---

34. Find a three-letter word that completes all three words on the left-hand side and prefixes all three words on the right-hand side.

PAR		EYE
HAT	(_ _ _)	HOT
MAR		DEN

---

35. Fill in the missing letters to name a group of ducks.

_ A _ D _ I _ G

---

36. What is the opposite of PIETY?

(A) SOLACE
(B) HOLINESS
(C) GOODNESS
(D) IRREVERENCE
(E) PASSION

---

37. Find a twelve-letter fruit made up of two six-letter words.

One word inside
One word outside

---

38. Place two of the three-letter groups together to make a six-letter vehicle.

OPY - SED - WAG - ONE - JAL - ANN

39. The vowels have been omitted from this quotation. See if you can put them back in.

THFMLYTHTPRYST
GTHRSTYSTGTHR

40. What number should replace the question mark?

TEST 8

1. What comes next?

?

A   B   C   D

---

2. What number is missing from the left-hand circle?

3. Add one letter, not necessarily the same letter, to each word to find two words that are opposite in meaning.

SEND HARD

---

4. Pair the eight words below to form four longer words.

IRON, LOAD, FIRE, WORK, MAIN, GRID, WOOD, LAND

5. Find the number to replace the question mark.

369542 is to 246359 as
172896 is to 268179 as
417638 is to ?

6. What do these words have in common?

LIBERATION   CHINCHILLA   INITIALLY   SPEARMINT
FRAGRANCE   PERFUME   CLAUSTROPHOBIA

7. What letter should replace the question mark?

18	4	22
S	E	?
7	21	3

8. Insert the letters of the phrase AN AGENT'S GAMMA into the following blanks only once each to complete a palindromic sentence, that is, one that reads the same backwards and forwards. For example, MADAM, I'M ADAM.

_ _ T _ _ _ _ ' _ _ _ _ E _ _ _

Clue: *Doorkeeper's ID*

9. DAWN is to DAY as WINTER is to:

AUTUMN, SEASON, NIGHT, SPRING, SUMMER

10. What phrase is indicated here?

O
V
E
R

11. What number should replace the question mark?

2	3	4	2
6	1	4	4
4	2	2	5
5	3	7	**?**

12. Solve the clues to find four six-letter words. The same three letters are represented by XYZ in each word.

XYZ _ _ _   **Clue:** *Falls*
_ XYZ _ _   **Clue:** *Hangs fabric*
_ _ XYZ _   **Clue:** *Graze*
_ _ _ XYZ   **Clue:** *Snare*

13. Which two words that sound alike but are spelled differently mean: SOLITARY, ADVANCE?

14. What are the missing letters:

15. Fill in the missing word in the crossword below:

16. Which is the odd one out?

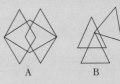

A   B

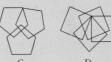

C   D

17. Which is the odd word out?

COMPRESS   DIMINISH
EBB   VANISH
DEPLETE

18. Fill in the consonants to complete four words that have the same meaning.

_ E _ E _ O U _
_ _ A _ I _ A _ L _
_ E _ E _ O _ E _ _
_ I _ _

Clue: *Openhanded*

19. Move from letter to letter horizontally and vertically, but not diagonally, to spell out a twelve-letter word. You have to find the starting point and provide the missing letters.

	M	M	E
R	I		N
I	S	O	

20. Place the letters in the grid to make a warm-blooded and a cold-blooded animal.

A A E K L L M S T

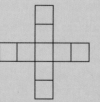

21. Which four-letter word placed inside the parentheses will complete these words?

(_ _ _ _) RAL E   (_ _ _ _) NT

22. Place two of the four-letter groups together to make a word.

TURN - EFUL - TACE - WACK - SPIT - INGS

23. Which word will carry on the sequence?

HALF-MAST, TAVERNER, RIPARIAN, NOBILITY, YULETIDE, ?

(A) DOUBLOON
(B) EXCITING
(C) MACARONI
(D) OVERTONE
(E) SKY PILOT
(F) TICKLISH

24. Find a six-letter word made up of only the following four letters.

A J
M P

25. Change this fraction to a decimal.

$$\frac{7}{8} =$$

26. LEG is to FIBULA as ARM is to:

(A) COCCYX
(B) THORAX
(C) CLAVICLE
(D) ULNA
(E) SCAPULA

27. Rearrange the two five-letter words to form a ten-letter word meaning "kind to strangers."

HABIT POLES

28. Which of the following is associated with HASLET?

(A) PATE
(B) BREAD
(C) ENTRAILS
(D) KIPPERS
(E) GINGER

29. Which word can be placed on the end of these words to make new words?

PILL
POT
GARB   (_ _ _)
FOOT
DAM

30. What is the symbol for CHROMIUM?

(A) C   (D) Cm
(B) Ch   (E) Chm
(C) Cr

31. Fill in the missing letters to name a group of cats.

_ L _ T _ E _

32. Fill in the missing letters to spell out different foods.

_ A _ B _ R _ E _
_ I _ C _ M _ A _
_ P _ G _ E _ T _

33. What does OROGRAPHY deal with?

(A) DESERTS   (D) MOUNTAINS
(B) TREES   (E) CAVES
(C) LAKES

34. Make up four pairs of words to find the odd one.

TOKEN   ICE   GREEN   SQUARE   SALTS
PEPPERS   FLOE   MAGIC   BATH

35. What is associated with GNOCCHI?

(A) SARDINES   (C) MELONS   (E) DUMPLINGS
(B) STRAWBERRIES   (D) TAPIOCA

36. To what does the adjective DIACONAL refer?

(A) DIAMOND SHAPED   (C) TEACHER   (E) WEALTH
(C) CONVERSATION   (D) DEACON

37. DELTIOLOGY is the study of

(A) RIVER MOUTHS   (C) BRIDGES   (E) FINGERS
(B) PICTURE POSTCARDS   (D) PRISONS

38. One man can mow a lawn in 6 hours, and another man can mow the same lawn in 3 hours. If they both worked together at their respective rates, how long would they take?

39. PISSIFORM is to PEA SHAPED as CLAVIFORM is to:

(A) CROSS SHAPED   (C) CLUB SHAPED   (E) SWORD SHAPED
(B) WEB SHAPED   (D) SQUARE SHAPED

40. What number should replace the question mark?

  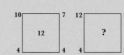

TEST 9

1. Divide the square into four equal sections so that each section contains the same three symbols twice.

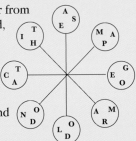

2. Take one letter from each circle and, reading clockwise, spell out an eight-letter word meaning "escort." You have to find the starting point.

3. What number comes next in this sequence?

0, 0, 1, 3, 6, 6, 7, 9, 12, 12, 13, ?

4. Arrange the words into the correct order and say whether the resulting statement is true or false.

LOVE WAS CUPID GREEK THE OF GOD

5. How many minutes before 10 AM is it if 90 minutes later it will be as many minutes after 11 AM?

6. Seven synonyms of the keyword are shown. Take one letter from each of the synonyms in order to spell out an eighth synonym of the keyword. **Keyword:** *METHOD*

SYNONYMS: FORM, MANNER, COURSE, SCHEME, ROUTINE, MODE, PLAN

7. Insert the name of a U.S. city into the bottom line to complete the three-letter words.

N	A	M	O	T	S	C	W	B
I	C	I	B	A	A	A	O	A

8. If 9L of a C is 9 lives of a cat, can you decode the following?

90D in an R.A.

9. How many more circles of the same size as the one already placed to the right will completely cover the square?

10. Create two words using each of the ten letters only once:

HIRBOMEDPA   **Clue:** *Macabre mountain*

11. Insert the letters provided into each quadrant to form two nouns: one reading clockwise around the inner circle and one reading counterclockwise around the outer circle.

NE: FNOK
SE: NINI
SW: DTGA
NW: RUIN

12. Fill in the missing numbers.

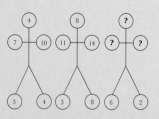

13. Start at a corner letter and spiral clockwise around the perimeter squares to spell out a nine-letter word that ends at the center square. You have to provide the missing letters.

C		I
S	M	T
I		I

14. What do these words have in common?

GLIMMER, CHORTLE, MOTEL, FLOUNDER

15. Which option continues the sequence below?

A   B   C   D

16. Place two four-letter groups together to make an eight-letter word that is a bone in the body.

ICLE - LLAN - PATE - SPHE - ILAC - CLAV

17. What number is two places away from itself plus 2, one place away from itself plus 5, two places away from itself less 3, and two places away from itself plus 1?

4	16	9	10
15	2	13	5
7	12	8	14
6	1	3	11

18. From these three words, find the two words that will form an anagram that is a synonym of the word remaining.

For example: LEG – MEEK – NET = MEEK – GENTLE (LEG + NET)

GAP – GALA – NEAT

19. What well-known phrase is indicated below?

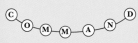

20. What is the meaning of the prefix GIGA?

(A) 10^5 (D) 10^8
(B) 10^6 (E) 10^9
(C) 10^7

21. Solve the cryptogram below. Each letter of the alphabet has been substituted with another.

KCSSAKK PK HAUUPBH NXDU FIC NDBU. XDGGPBAKK PK TPZPBH NXDU FIC HAU. —X. EDSZKIB LJINB

22. Place a word in the parentheses that when placed at the end of the first word makes a word and when placed in front of the second word also makes a word.

OPERA (_ _ _) US

23. Insert each of the letters of the phrase STAB DERRIERE into the grid only once to find two related words.
Clue: *Strike it rich!*

24. What type of animal is an ORYX?

(A) ANTELOPE
(B) MONKEY
(C) LLAMA
(D) RAT
(E) SHEEP

25. Place three of the two-letter groups together to form a tree.

SE - NK - SP - GO - GI - RU

26. Use each pair of letters once to form four four-letter vegetables—one pair is not used.

RA	ME	BE
LE	ET	LE
KA	EK	OK

27. Which of these is not an anagram of a dog?

(A) UAUACHHHI
(B) LLOPAPIN
(C) SNACHON
(D) HDNEKLOU
(E) LAUSKI
(F) GIROC

28. Find three birds hidden in this passage: "After the storm we must then fly the balloon at once; it will be awful."

29. If the missing letters in the two circles are correctly inserted, they will form synonymous words. The words do not have to be read in a clockwise direction, but the letters are consecutive. What are the words and missing letters?

30. What is always part of a DEMIJOHN?

(A) GREAT AGE
(B) GOLD CAP
(C) SQUARE BODY
(D) NARROW NECK
(E) BLUE LABEL

31. How many triangles are there in this figure?

32. What number should replace the question mark?

Simplify:
$8 - 6 \times 7 - 10 \div 5 + 1 = ?$

33. Which two words have opposite meanings?

DISORDER, IMMODEST, HEEDFUL, INFUSION, OBLIVIOUS, INNATE

34. Which circle's letters cannot be rearranged into a six-letter word?

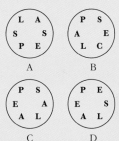

35. Find a seven-letter word by moving along the lines connecting the circles.

36. What number should continue the series?

4 7 9 8 7 5 6 9
5 7 5 ?

37. What word will fit in front of these words to make new words?

(_ _ _)

COAT
KNOT
HEAVY
SAIL
HAT

38. Find a twelve-letter animal made up of two six-letter words—one word inside, one word outside.

39. What number should replace the question mark?

219   208   186   ?   109   54   –12

40. Which word means the same as CHAGRIN?

(A) IDLENESS   (D) BENEFIT
(B) SMILING   (E) PENSIVE
(C) ANNOYANCE

TEST 10

1. What number should replace the question mark?

2. "The ability to exert effort for a purpose." What word below best fits this definition?

CAPABILITY
POTENTIAL
VIGOR
TALENT
POWER

3. Find a four-letter word that forms a different word with each preceding letter or letters.

C
L
SH
DR
H   (_ _ _ _)
R
CL
PL
M

4. What letter is missing from the pyramid?

5. Insert each of the letters in the phrase ESOTERIC DEVISE into the grid once to find two connected words.

Clue: *Elementary, my dear Watson!*

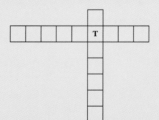

6. Simplify to find x:

$$\frac{-7 \times 3 \times 2}{3 \times 2 \times 7} = x$$

7. Which hexagon should replace the question mark?

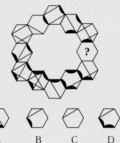

A   B   C   D

8. Which two words are opposite in meaning?

FLAT, CONCAVE, REVERSED, STRAIGHT, BULGING, EMPTY

9. Solve the three anagrams to produce a well-known quotation by Sir John Vanbrugh.

_ _ _ _ _ _ _ _ _ _ _ _

HUG SHALE   **SHOT WEB**

_ _ _ _ _ _ _ _ _ _

HALTS A SLUG

12. What is the value of the second line?

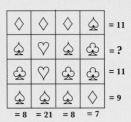

10. Choose a word from the right-hand column to accompany the words in the left-hand column.

INOPPORTUNE	AGLOW
DEFEAT	FIRST
ASTUTE	RIDDEN
CALMNESS	PLEASE
?	REMOTE

13. Find the starting point and track from letter to letter along the lines to spell out the name of an American river (eleven letters). There is one double-letter in the name.

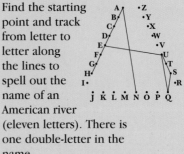

11. What number should replace the question mark?

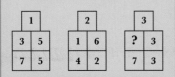

14. A familiar phrase has been split up and jumbled into three-letter groups. Find the saying. For example, FIND THE QUOTE could be jumbled up into DTH, OTE, FIN, EQU.

OPO, EWO, FTH, ONT, RLD

15. Each number has a choice of three letters. Dial an American writer (whose name has 8 and 5 letters): 32676722 77235

ABC **1**	DEF **2**	GHI **3**
JKL **4**	MNO **5**	PQR **6**
STU **7**	VWX **8**	YZ **9**
*	**0**	**#**

16. Take a letter from each tree in turn to spell out five types of tree.

17. Simplify: $\dfrac{1}{4} \div \dfrac{7}{8}$

18. What numbers should appear on the bottom row?

15	13	19	22
37	34	35	32
69	72	66	69
?	?	?	?

19. Which number is the odd one out?

5735 7428
9436 6848
4520
3927   5935
2918 9654
4832 8756
6318

20. Insert a word that completes the first word and starts the second.

DO (_ _ _) NECK

21. Complete the words to form names of animals. Then rearrange the initial letters of each word to find a sixth animal.

_ L _ N _
_ E _ N _ E _ R
_ E _ U
_ N _ E _ O _ E
_ U _ F _ L _

22. What is associated with DANCETTE?

(a) CIRCUS
(b) PUPPET
(c) CAROUSEL
(d) STATUE
(e) ZIGZAG

26. By moving through the doorways spell out an eight-letter word.

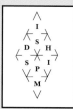

23. A company asked its workforce to increase production by 6% per week. If the employees worked a 5-day week, how much more would they need to produce each day to achieve the desired 6% weekly increase?

27. Fill in the blanks to find three boats.

```
_ E _ T _ O _ E _
_ I _ E _ A _ E _
_ R _ O _ S _ I _
```

28. Find the eight-letter word.

(1 2 3 4) HOLE - PAIN (5 6 7 8)
(6 5 1 4) _ _ _ _ _ _ _ _ (3 7 2 8)

24. Make one word using all ten letters.

SCOOP CRIME

Clue: *Scientific instrument*

29. What number should replace the question mark?

25. What is the name given to a group of WILDFOWL?

(a) PLUMP
(b) CLAMOUR
(c) CLUSTER
(d) WING
(e) CHATTERING
(f) BLAST

30. The library was selling off old books.

I purchased 12 for $12.

Some were 50¢, some were $1.50, some were $2.

How many of each did I buy?

31. How many degrees are there in this angle?

(a) 115°
(b) 120°
(c) 125°
(d) 130°
(e) 135°

32. Which is the odd one out?

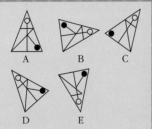

A   B   C

D   E

33. Which religious sign is the Greek cross?

(a)
(b)
(c)
(d)
(e)

34. Which word means the fear of FOOD?

(a) ARETEPHOBIA
(b) EOSOPHOBIA
(c) SITOPHOBIA
(d) GENOPHOBIA
(e) KINESOPHOBIA

35. "How heavy is this bag of rice?" I asked the shopkeeper. "128 lbs divided by half its weight," he said. How much did it weigh?

36. Place two of the three-letter groups together to form a tree.

LEA - UCE - CHI - ELA - SPR - LEN - PIN - BEE

37. Which temperature below is 68° Fahrenheit changed to Celsius?

(a) 18°C
(b) 19°C
(c) 20°C
(d) 21°C
(e) 22°C

38. What is the meaning of ARGOT?

(a) SILVER   (b) NUBILE   (c) GOLD INGOT   (d) GOODS   (e) SLANG

39. Trace out a ten-letter word in any direction, using each letter once only.

40. In how many different ways can the Olympic rings be arranged in color order?

TEST 11

1. If meat in a river (3 in 6) is T(HAM)ES, can you find frozen rain in a country (4 in 8)?

2. Insert the missing consonants to complete a magic square where all words read the same across and down.

B, L, D, G, S, D, D, R, L, R, B, T, D, T

		A		E
	I		E	
A		I		I
	E		I	
E		I		

3. You are looking for one word in this paragraph. The word appears only once, its first letter being the eighth letter after a certain vowel. The same vowel is the tenth letter to appear after its last letter. What is the word?

4. What number is missing from the third hexagon?

5. Which is the odd one out?

PATELLA, FIBULA, RADIUS, FEMUR, TIBIA

6. TANS = 8
CAVE = 9
LEAF = 12
TAX = ?

9. Which comes next?

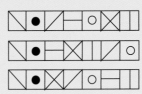

?

A. B. C. D.

7. Change FIRE to WATER. The asterisks in each word are common to the word above it.

```
     F I R E
 _ _ * * _ _ _ _ _ _
     _ _ * * * * _ _ _
       _ _ * * * * _ _
         * * * _ _ _
     _ _ _ _ _ _ _
         _ * * _ _ _ _ _
           * *
         _ _ _ _
       W A T E R
```

Clue: *Declaration*
Clue: *Tend*
Clue: *Inciter*
Clue: *Line on map*
Clue: *Position*

10. Solve the cryptic clue below. The answer is a thirteen-letter anagram contained within the clue.

NURSE I SPY GYPSIES RUN WHEN I'M ON RAPID CALL.

8. What number should replace the question mark?

11. Complete the three hyphenated words:

_ _ _ _ T – H _ _ E – B _ _ _ _

Clue: *Lack of success*

---

12. Which figure continues the sequence below?

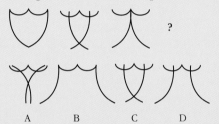

?

A　　B　　C　　D

---

13. Eliminate twelve letters from the phrase below to leave a word meaning "shakes."

READ BETWEEN THE LINES

---

14. POST- : LATER
MACRO- :

LATE
LANGUAGE
SMALL
LARGE
LAST

---

15. What number should replace the question mark?
Simplify: $6 - 3 \times 2 + 8 \div 4 + 6 = ?$

---

16. What number should replace the question mark?

---

17. Which is the odd one out?

A　　B　　C　　D

---

18. A train traveling at a speed of 40 mph enters a tunnel that is $1\frac{1}{4}$ miles long. The length of the train is $\frac{1}{4}$ mile. How long does it take for all of the train to pass through the tunnel, from the moment the front enters to the moment the rear emerges?

19. Place two letters in each pair of parentheses so that they finish the word on the left and start the word on the right. Reading across, combine these pairs to spell out a six-letter musical word.

LE (_ _) D   WI (_ _) IN   G (_ _) IT

20. Which is the odd one out?

A   B   C   D

21. In this square, what is the product of the largest prime number multiplied by the smallest even number?

8	41	83
53	10	67
71	11	6

22. GAGGLE is to GEESE as POD is to

(a) FLAMINGOS   (b) CROCODILES   (c) BEARS
(d) WHALES   (e) SPIDERS

23. Simplify $\dfrac{175}{1000}$ as a fraction.

24. BEDROOMS, ROMANTIC, ANSWERED, WEAKENED, ?
Which is the next word?
KEYBOARD, ABDICATE, CATACOMB, KILOBYTE

25. What is the meaning of FAUCET?
(a) HAT   (b) TAP
(c) MASK   (d) FOUNTAIN
(e) DOCK

26. Find a six-letter word made up of only the following four letters.
O M I N

27. DANCER is to RHUMBA as SINGER is to

(a) BASSOON
(b) POLKA
(c) COULOMB
(d) DOTTEREL
(e) MADRIGAL

28. Place four of the three-letter groups together to make two six-letter words.

ATO - PIN - WRE - ILE - SEN - ATH - NSH - DON

29. Place a word in the parentheses that when placed on the end of the first word makes a word and when placed in front of the second word also makes a word.

DESSERT (_ _ _ _ _) BILL

30. Fill in the blanks to find words to do with building.

A		T		C
S				Y
E		E		T

31. Complete the word that contains these middle letters.

_ _ _ NGIP _ _ _

32. Find a one-word anagram from the two words below.

SANE DOSE

33. What is the mathematical sign for summation?

(a) Π
(b) Σ
(c) $\approx$
(d) ✿
(e) ◊

34. Which two words are similar in meaning?

AWKWARD
BRISK
GAMIN
TEAM
SPORTSMAN
URCHIN

35. Place the letters in the grid to make a shell and a weapon.

A C C C E
H L N O

36. What is the opposite of ESPOUSE?

(a) OPPOSE (b) WELCOME
(c) DISMAY (d) HUSBAND
(e) INFORM

37. Complete the sequence.

A
17

D
21

G
26

?
?

38. Fill in the missing letters to complete the word.

_ _ _ CHW _ _ _

39. Which word can be placed on the end of these words to make new words?

WAS
WIT
ZIT (_ _ _)
FAT
GAT

40. Rearrange the two words to form a nine-letter word meaning a "type of shellfish."

PART GOODS

TEST 12

1. Solve the anagram in parentheses to complete the quotation correctly.

(Gain into aim) is the eye of the soul.

—Joubert

2. Which line of figures is the odd one out?

3. What phrase is indicated here?

7. What number should replace the question mark?

4. 59 is to 98 as 65 is to

59, 86, 89, 56

8. Find three words starting with the letters OPP that are opposite in meaning to the words given:

A. LIBERATE = OPP _ _ _ _
B. CONCURRENCE = OPP _ _ _ _ _ _ _
C. UNTIMELY = OPP _ _ _ _ _ _

5. Add one letter, not necessarily the same letter, to each word in the front, end, or middle to find two words that are opposite in meaning.

ALLY, ROSE

9. Read clockwise to find a ten-letter word. You must find the starting point and provide the missing letters. The word you are looking for starts and finishes with the same two letters.

E D
M
O L
E

6. Some widgets are brown. Everything brown has a straight edge. Therefore, which of the following must be true?

A. All widgets have a straight edge.
B. Everything brown is a widget.
C. Some widgets have a straight edge.

10. Alter one letter in each of the words below to form four new words of the same theme.

BALL, HARM, CUTE, FINE

11. Which is the missing section?

A   B

C   D

12. What number should replace the question mark?

①

③ ⑨ ⑦

⑤

③

⑦ ⑲ ⑮

⑪

②

⑤ ⑭ ⑪

⑧

④

⑨ ? ⑲

⑭

13. Which word is closest in meaning to FRETFUL?

GUILTY, PETULANT, UNNERVED, DISMAYED, FRANTIC

14. Insert each of the letters of the phrase ELFIN LENSES once in the spaces below to complete a palindromic sentence—that is, one that reads the same backwards and forwards. For example, MADAM, I'M ADAM.

_ _ _ I _ _ _ _ _ _ _ E _

Clue: *Old toms*

15. How many lines appear below?

16. Find the complete word that contains these middle letters. The word is hyphenated.

_ _ PPLEG _ _ _

17. Find five words starting at the top of the pyramid and taking one letter from each row in turn. Every letter in the pyramid is used at least once.

G

R U

E A I

D P N A

E D T H O

18. Match each word in column A with a related word in column B.

A	B
SHEET	TURN
LAPEL	WRITE
NUT	WRAP
PAPER	CRACK

19. What is the missing section?

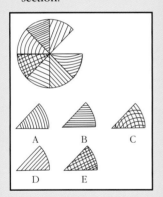

A   B   C

D   E

21. Insert the name of a tree into the bottom line to complete the three-letter words.

H	S	P	P	T	A	S	T
E	P	E	I	O	I	K	E

22. What number should replace the question mark?

27   $28\frac{1}{2}$ $31\frac{1}{2}$?   42 $49\frac{1}{2}$ $58\frac{1}{2}$

23. If the missing letters in the circle are correctly inserted they will form an eight-letter word. The word does not have to be read in a clockwise direction, but the letters are consecutive. What is the word and missing letters?

20. In a horse race the first five places were filled by Horses 3, 7, 18, 9, and 16. The jockey of Horse 3 wore a crimson shirt, the jockey of Horse 7 wore green, jockey 18 wore red, and 9 wore ivory. What color did the jockey of Horse 16 wear? Was it yellow, purple, black, or maroon?

24. What number in the decimal system is represented by this binary notation?

1100110   (a) 56
            (b) 98
            (c) 100
            (d) 102
            (e) 104

25. What is a slice across a cone that is not parallel to, or does not pass through, the base called?

(a) CYCLOID
(b) HYPERBOLA
(c) PARABOLA
(d) ELLIPSE

26. Which mathematical symbol should replace the question mark to continue the series?

× – + ÷ × – + ÷ × ?

27. Place a word in the parentheses that when placed on the end of the first word makes a word, and when placed in front of the second word also makes a word.

SAND (_ _ _) GAIN

28. This is a treasure map. The treasure is marked T. You have to find the starting square. 2N means move 2 squares north.

N

T	1E	2S	3W
3E	1S	1W	2S
1S	2E	2W	2N
2E	3N	2N	2W

W   E

S

29. If 6 × 4 = 26, then 5 × 4 = ?

30. What number replaces the question mark?

15 1 $10\frac{3}{4}$ $3\frac{1}{8}$ $6\frac{1}{2}$ $5\frac{1}{4}$?

31. What is the name given to a group of SNIPE?

(a) GATHERING
(b) SPRING
(c) TUFT
(d) STALK
(e) GAME
(f) WISP

32. Place two of the four-letter groups together to make a word.

RBID - VIRT - WHAC - UNDE - UOSA - INGS

33. Which of these is not a fruit?

(a) KUMQUAT   (c) PEARMAIN   (e) MUSCATEL
(b) ANANAS   (d) TAMARIND   (f) EPHEMERA

34. Find the three fish hidden in this sentence: "When you have played the red ace, change limits to perhaps one pound per point."

35. Rearrange the letters in each circle to form two seven-letter words that are synonyms. Each word commences with the center letter.

36. Which temperature below is 15° Celsius changed to Fahrenheit?

(a) 58°F   (b) 59°F   (c) 60°F   (d) 61°F   (e) 62°F

37. The vowels have been omitted from this quotation. See if you can insert them back in.

WNNNGSNTVRTHNGTSTHNLTHNG

38. Make one word using all ten letters.

STRIDE CHAP   **Clue:** *Sender*

39. Find a twelve-letter insect made of two six-letter words, one word inside, one word outside.

40. Starting at an outside square and moving in any direction, spell out the name of a ten-letter continent

DA	CA	AN
TI	MB	TA
OD	RC	IA

TEST 13

1. Six antonyms of the keyword are shown. Take one letter from each of the six antonyms to spell out a seventh antonym of the keyword.

Keyword: OUTSET

Antonyms: FINISH, CLOSING, END, TERMINATION, CONCLUSION, COMPLETION

2. Which is the odd pair of letters?

BY, HS, EV, JR, GT

4. What famous European landmark is indicated here?

R	F	A
A	A	R
G	L	T

3. Insert a word that finishes the first word and starts the second.

DAM		ANT

5. What comes next in the sequence below?

?

A.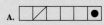

B.

C.

D.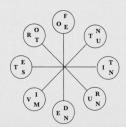

6. Take one letter from each circle and, reading clockwise, spell out an eight-letter word meaning "solemn." You have to find the starting point.

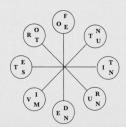

7. Fill in the missing letters to complete the word below:

_ I _ I _ I _ I _ I _ Y

Clue: *Shares*

8. What number should replace the question mark?

2	6	3	3	8	5
9	5	6	2	9	7
4	6	1	6	9	2
2	1	9	7	5	8
7	9	1	2	9	6
4	1	7	8	?	3

9. Take one word from each column to make four compound words. For example: the five words DOOR, STEP, SON, NET, WORK would produce the words: DOORSTEP, STEPSON, SONNET, NETWORK.

A	B	C	D	E
PORT	SOME	ON	HOPE	BORN
FEAR	TIME	DUMB	EVER	MORE
PART	LESS	MOON	NEW	FREE
SING	ABLE	WHERE	STRUCK	GREEN
OVER	LET	SHARE	COST	LESS

10. Rearrange the two five-letter words to find a ten-letter word meaning "two-masted vessel."

BRAIN TINGE

11. What continues the sequence?

A   B

C   D

13. "To consider or examine attentively or deliberately." Which word below does *not* fit this definition?

MEDIATE
PONDER
RUMINATE
REFLECT
DELIBERATE

14. Make PIE HUMBLE by following these instructions:

PIE
1. Change a letter: _ _ _
2. Change a letter: _ _ _
3. Change a letter: _ _ _
4. Add three letters: HUMBLE

12. All the following words relate to meetings: CAUCUS, AUDIENCE, ENCOUNTER, FORUM, RALLY, SEMINAR, SYNOD, SUMMIT, CONFERENCE. Match each of the words with its correct definition below:

(i) Casual and unplanned
(ii) Discussion of a specialized academic theme
(iii) Public discussion
(iv) Local political party to decide policy
(v) Conference between heads of government
(vi) Exchange of views or securing advice
(vii) Formal meeting with VIP
(viii) Public assembly for a political cause
(ix) Meeting or council of church officials

15. What word can be placed on the end of these words to make new words?

CHIN
BLAME
PAIN (_ _ _ _)
COLOR
HARM

16. Move from star to star to spell out a ten-letter phrase (word lengths = 2, 2, 1, 5).

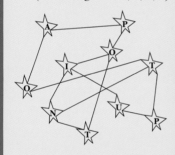

17. BADGER (ABIDE) PIERCE
Using the same rules as the above example, what word should appear in the parentheses below?

NECTAR (_ _ _ _ _) CARPET

18. When this shape is folded to form a cube, just one of the following can be produced. Which one?

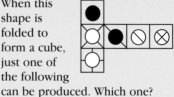

A   B   C   D

19. Make up four pairs of words and find the odd one.

CRAZY   MEATY   POST
APPLE   FIRST   TURNOVER
SEAS   GANG   CHINA

20. Insert the missing word in the crossword below:

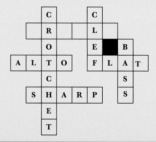

21. Simplify $\dfrac{925}{1000}$ as a fraction.

22. Find the missing square.

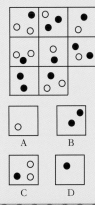

A   B

C   D

23. 3 apples + 4 bananas cost 29¢, and 1 apple + 8 bananas cost 43¢. How much is 1 banana?

24. How many minutes is it before 12:00 noon if 70 minutes ago it was four times as many minutes past 9:00 AM?

25. Complete the five words so that two letters are common to each word—i.e., the same two letters that end the first word also start the second word, and so on. The two letters that end the fifth word are the first two letters of the first word, thus completing the association.

_ _ N A _ _
_ _ D I _ _
_ _ P I _ _
_ _ C E _ _
_ _ B T _ _

26. Rearrange the letters in each circle to find two seven-letter words that are synonyms. Each word commences with the central letter.

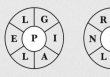

27. Place three of the two-letter groups together to form a card game.

PO - PI - RI - ET - KE - QU

28. Which figure below carries on the sequence?

   **?**

A   B   C   D   E   F

29. Change this fraction to a decimal: $\frac{1}{16}$.

30. Fill in the missing letters to make a nine-letter word, starting from a corner square and continuing in a spiral to the center.

F		O
U	E	T
	C	A

31. Which two words have opposite meanings?

VIVACIOUS, INDIFFERENCE, TRIBULATION, HAPPINESS, SARCASM, DISTRACTION

32. If the missing letters in the two circles are correctly inserted they will form synonymous words. The words do not have to be read in a clockwise direction, but the letters are consecutive. What are the words and missing letters?

33. Which of the following is always associated with FLAVIN?

(a) YELLOW
(b) BLUE
(c) PINK
(d) MAUVE
(e) WHITE

34. Moving through the doorways spell out an eight-letter word.

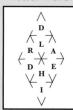

35. Fill in the blanks to form different sports.

```
_ A _ M _ N _ O _
_ R _ S _ L _ N _
_ I _ L _ A _ D _
```

36. What number should replace the question mark?

Simplify: $10 + 12 \div 4 + 2 \times 9 - 10 = ?$

37. Which two words are similar in meaning?

STRAINED, VERBOSE, BASIC, DULCET, DISPOSES, SWEET

38. Which word means the fear of dogs?

(a) KOPOPHOBIA   (c) LALIOPHOBIA   (e) CYNOPHOBIA
(b) PYROPHOBIA   (d) STASIPHOBIA

39. Complete the three words below that have these countries in them: WALES, CHAD, ITALY

```
_ W A _ _ L E S
_ _ C H A _ D
_ _ I T _ A L _ Y
```

40. What is the meaning of IDEOLOGY?

(a) IDOLATRY
(b) TRADE
(c) BELIEFS
(d) IDEALS
(e) COMMERCE

TEST 14

1.   **?**

A   B   C   D

What continues the above sequence?

2. What phrase is indicated below?

_ _ A V I _ _

3. What letter is missing from the wall?

H	N	E	E
R		T	E	O
T	M	O	O
D	R	A	R	Y
O	G	W	?

4. What number should replace the question mark?

5. Which two words are the odd ones out?

UNFOLD
SWEARS EFFETE
AIL DEPART
FEE NOD
PURSUE USE
FACIAL DUE
DOUSE EAT
WAS LID ALLIED
TRUISM RIM

6. Arrange the words into the correct order; then say whether the resulting statement is true or false.

KNOWN ETRUSCANS ANCIENT CENTRAL THE AREA NOW CALLED THE INHABITANTS IN TUSCANY WERE AS OF ITALY

7. Which is the missing section?

8. A car travels 20 miles in the same time as another car, traveling 20 mph faster, covers 30 miles. How long does the journey take?

9. Find the starting point and track from letter to letter along the lines to spell out a sixteen-letter phrase (8-3-5).

There are two sets of double letters in the phrase, including one that ends a word and starts the next.

10. Place two of the three-letter groups together to form an animal.

TIG - HOR - SEL - SEN - SHE - WEA - ERA - EPA

11. Each number has a choice of three letters. Dial an explorer (word lengths = 5, 8): 65142 15752725

12. What number should replace the question mark?

763	219	37
435	367	95
256	?	28

13. Arrange these words into four groups with each group containing three related words.

ASIDE, WISE, BACK, ZONE, DISC, MINE, BOMB, WORK, SAIL, TOWER, SCALE, RUSH

Clue: *Set time on gold clock*

14. On a shopping spree at Macy's, my wife spent half the money in her purse within 15 minutes. This meant she was left with as many cents as she had dollars before, and half as many dollars as she had cents before. How much money did she originally have?

15. Find the starting point and visit every square to reach the treasure marked T.

1N 2W =
1 North 2 West

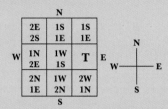

16. Which is the missing square?

A   B   C

17. What number should replace the question mark?

2   12 $5\frac{1}{4}$ $9\frac{3}{4}$ $8\frac{1}{2}$ $7\frac{1}{2}$?

18. Insert two words that are anagrams of each other to complete the sentence. For example: She removed the *stain* from her new *satin* dress.

A _____ fisherman, he knew exactly the right spot on the riverbank for some rich pickings. Sure enough, within a few moments he had on his face a look of pure satis-faction as the fish began to _____ into his net.

19. In the arrangement of numbers below, what is the difference between the sum of the two highest prime numbers and the product of the two lowest square numbers?

8	23	3	49
19	4	29	17
37	25	35	16

20. Only ten letters of the alphabet do not appear in this grid. What ten-letter phrase can these ten letters be used to spell out?

Clue: *Slapstick*

J	Q	F	B
O	Z	K	G
N	W	Y	M
X	H	L	V

21. TURQUOISE : BLUE
JASPER :

YELLOW
RED
ORANGE
BROWN
GREEN

22. A well-known phrase has had all its vowels removed and has been split into groups of three letters. What is the phrase? All remaining letters are in the correct order.

MTL DMR TNS CTY

23. Which is the odd one out?

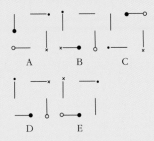

A   B   C

D   E

24. Unravel the logic behind this diagram to find which symbol should go into the square with the question mark.

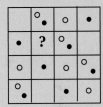

25. What word will fit in front of these words to form new words?

         HEART
         BREAD
(_ _ _ _ _) TOOTH
         WILLIAM
         NESS

26. Find the eight-letter word.

DINE – COMA
(1234) (5678)

– – – – – – – –
(5 6 7 4)(1 2 8 3)

27. What number should replace the question mark?

28. What is struck when a glockenspiel is played?

(a) BARS   (d) CYMBALS
(b) STRINGS (e) DRUMS
(c) PIANO

29. A word can be placed in the parentheses that has the same meaning as the words outside. What is it? Each dash represents a letter.

THIN METAL (_ _ _ _) THWART

30. What is the mathematical sign for square root?

(a) ≠
(b) □
(c) *f*
(d) √
(e) ″

31. Which word means the same as MAWKISH?

(a) UGLY
(b) GROTESQUE
(c) INSIPID
(d) EVIL
(e) DASTARDLY

32. Place the letters in the grid to make drums and a boat.

ABCGENOOO

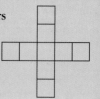

33. HARDWOOD is to APPLE as SOFTWOOD is to:

(a) FIR   (d) OAK
(b) BEECH (e) WILLOW
(c) PALM

34. If you were riding a HINNY, it would be the offspring of a:

(a) PONY + AN ASS
(b) HEIFER + A DONKEY
(c) STALLION + A SHE ASS
(d) PONY + A DONKEY
(e) ASS + A DONKEY

35. Fill in the missing letters to name a group of horses.

_ A _ R _ S

36. Which circle's letters cannot be rearranged into a six-letter word?

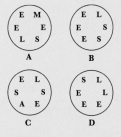

37. Find a one-word anagram made up of these letters.

LEMON ODE

38. Find a twelve-letter vegetable made up of two six-letter words—one inside the star, one outside the star.

39. Combine pairs of letters to form four four-letter biblical characters—one pair is not used.

IN	EL	NO
AM	AH	AD
AB	AC	CA

40. Find the complete word that contains these middle letters. The word is hyphenated.

_ _ R F E T C _ _ _

TEST 15

1. Which is the odd one out?

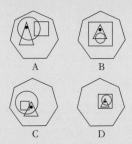

A   B

C   D

2. Working counterclockwise, take one letter from each circle to spell out two antonyms.

Note: *Each word starts in a different circle.*

3. TITANIC VEER is an anagram of what eleven-letter word?

4. Which is the odd one out?

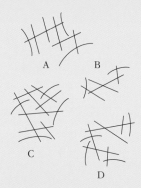

5. Imagine two bags. Each bag contains eight balls: four white balls, and four black balls. A ball is drawn out of Bag 1 and another ball out of Bag 2. What are the chances that at least one of the balls will be black?

A. 1 chance in 4
B. 1 chance in 2
C. 2 chances in 3
D. 3 chances in 4

6. Which figure below fits into the vacant space?

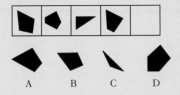

A   B   C   D

7. What two numbers can you place before all the three-digit numbers below so that all resulting five-digit numbers are divisible by 7?

       976
       661
_ _   381
       864
       927

8. JAVELIN, MODULAR, LEXICON, MUTATED, ?

What word below continues the above sequence?

LIBERAL
BAROQUE
VOLUTED
LINOCUT
VENISON

9. Eliminate thirteen letters from the phrase below to leave a word meaning "suggested."

HIT THE NAIL ON THE HEAD

10. 786395 : 658793
941682 :

     124968
     142986
     124986
     129486
     214986

11. What do these words have in common?

RESTRAINED, DWINDLE, COUNTERSUNK, SKILLIGALEE

12. I am nine-letters long: 123456789.

My first four "1234" is to recognize.

My last five "56789" is a ridge.

My last four "6789" is a boundary.

What am I?

13. Where would you put the number 10 in the grid?

1				8	
2		6			
3	5				
				9	
4			7		

14. Complete the following (two words):

_ A _ A _ _ A _ A _

Clue: *Isthmus*

15. Add three consecutive letters of the alphabet to the group of letters below to form a seven-letter word.

FILY

17. Which two words are opposite in meaning?

AFFIRM, DELAY, RECANT, REFER, CHANGE, OBLITERATE

18. What word is indicated below?

19. "A movement or course having a particular direction and character." Which word below does <u>not</u> fit this definition?

CURRENT, TENOR, TENDENCY, VOGUE, DRIFT

20. Find a letter that replaces the question mark.

116 (O), 672 (S), 499 (F), 271 (?)

16. Eight square pieces of paper, all exactly the same size, have been placed on top of each other so that some part of each piece of paper can be seen. Sheet A is shown completely and was, therefore, the last piece of paper to be placed. Which was the first piece of paper to be placed? Can this fact be determined?

B	F	
	C	A
G	E	D
		H

21. Which word is the odd one out?

BLITHERING
CATHEDRAL
WAREHOUSE
PROMETHEAN
STEPMOTHER

22. What number should replace the question mark?

23. Which word should carry on the sequence?

GRUMBLE, EYELASH, HOLDALL, LOCKNUT, TARRING, ?

(a) SKIMMED
(b) MIDLAND
(c) CLEAVER
(d) DUCTILE
(e) GRAPHIC
(f) HOLIDAY

24. What color is CINNABAR?
(a) PURPLE   (d) BLUE
(b) BLACK   (e) VERMILLION
(c) YELLOW

25. Simplify $\dfrac{1}{7} \div \dfrac{9}{14}$.

26. What is the meaning of ERUDITE?
(a) BULKY
(b) EFFERVESCENT
(c) SIMPLE
(d) LEARNED
(e) LOGICAL

27. If GAGGLE is to GEESE, then MURDER is to:

(a) EAGLES
(b) PELICANS
(c) SWALLOWS
(d) CHAFFINCHES
(e) CROWS

28. Place four of the three-letter groups together to make two six-letter words.

LEG – LAW – GLE – END –
OUT – GIN – DED - MIS

29. Which of these is not an anagram of a ruler?

    (a) MAZIN   (c) PHILCA   (e) ZAWRI

    (b) DRARIS   (d) HALLMU   (f) GLIOATNI

---

30. Which two words have opposite meanings?

IGNOMINY, PASTICHE, COMPROMISE, HUNGER, NICTITATE, HONOR

---

31. Find a six-letter word made up of only the following four letters.

E N L K

---

32. What number should replace the question mark?

---

33. Place two three-letter groups together to make a six-letter word that is a cabin.

EPE - TEP - ANA - LAT - CAB - CHA

---

34. Which of these is not a fish?

    (a) MOIDORE   (c) WRASSE   (e) TURBOT

    (b) HALIBUT   (d) FLOUNDER   (f) LAMPREY

35. What letter should replace the question mark?

B	V	J	N	R
Z	F	R	N	?

36. What is the opposite of SONOROUS?

(a) SLEEPY
(b) CAREFUL
(c) PHLEGMATIC
(d) FEEBLE
(e) SOFT

37. Rearrange the letters in each hexagon to find two seven-letter words that are synonyms. Both words commence with the central letter.

38. What is the name given to a group of MARTENS?

(a) EARTH
(b) ERST
(c) CLUTTER
(d) RICHNESS
(e) FLIGHT
(f) THICKET

39. Starting at an outside square and moving in any direction, spell out the ten-letter name of a tree.

IL	PT	LY
US	CA	KT
EU	BL	AC

40. HOTEL is to WAITER as CIRCUS is to:

(a) TROUBADOUR
(b) LASCAR
(c) GRINGO
(d) FUNAMBULIST
(e) TOREADOR

TEST 16

1.

is to 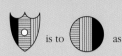 as

 is to

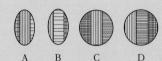

A   B   C   D

2. Which two words are opposite in meaning?

MALICE, BRAVERY, ECSTASY, OPPRESSION, PRESTIGE, SUPPORT

3. Insert each of the letters from the phrase **IDEAS LOCATED** into the grid once to find two connected words.

Clue: *Satanic supporter*

4. What two numbers have the same relationship as 5963 : 810?

A. 7219 : 126
B. 5698 : 804
C. 2729 : 72
D. 1520 : 3040
E. 1234 : 765

5. Insert each of the letters from the words ONE DON REVVED once into the spaces below to complete a palindromic sentence—that is, one that reads the same backwards and forwards. For example: MADAM, I'M ADAM.

_ _ _ _ _ _ _ _ _ R _ _ E _

6. What phrase is indicated below?

7. Which pair of letters is the odd one out?

IQ   TF
LN   OK   JP
WC   HP

8. What number should replace the question mark?

9. Complete the words to find five colors or shades. The initial letters of each word can then be arranged to spell out a sixth color or shade.

_ N _ I _ O
_ M _ E _
_ A _ E _ D _ R
_ R _ A _
_ E _ O _

10. Which two words that sound alike, but are spelled differently, mean: LEND, SOLITARY?

11. What letter should replace the question mark?

12.

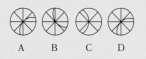

What contains the above sequence?

A   B   C   D

13. The words "in" and "out" are antonyms. Find two other words, one rhyming with "in" and one rhyming with "out," that are also antonyms.

14. What letter is two to the right of the letter immediately to the left of the letter three to the right of the letter immediately to the left of the letter C?

15. Three members of an ex-wives club were comparing notes. "I was married to James for just 9 months," said Trixie. "That's longer than me," said Davinia. "I walked out on him after 6 months." "Looks like I should have the prize for endurance then," said Helen. For how many months was she married to her husband?

16. Read around the track in the direction of the arrow to find a fifteen-letter word. The overlapping letter appears twice. You must provide the missing letters.

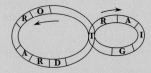

17. Which is the odd one out?

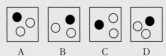

A   B   C   D

18. Add one letter, not necessarily the same letter, to each word to find two words that are similar in meaning.

EARN LOG

19. All of the following words relate to business. Match up the words with their closest definitions below.

FLOTATION, INTANGIBLE, SYNDIC, FACTOR, TRANSACTION, LOGO, INCORPORATE, FLYER, MONOPOLY, FLAGSHIP

(i) Launching a business by means of a share issue
(ii) Trademark symbol or emblem
(iii) Exclusive control over a business activity
(iv) Deal
(v) Agent
(vi) Asset that has a value but no physical existence
(vii) Form into a registered company
(viii) Most impressive or successful product
(ix) Risky venture
(x) Representative, as of a university

20. Which is the odd one out?

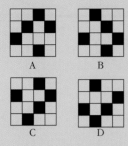

A   B

C   D

21. Change the fraction to a decimal.

$$\frac{5}{16} =$$

22. What is the meaning of SHRIKE?

(a) SHRINK
(b) VEGETABLE
(c) BIRD
(d) FISH
(e) DICE GAME

23. The vowels have been omitted from this quotation. Can you replace them?

THLNTCSHVTKNCHRGFTHSLM

24. Z A P Y A W W H Y G U Y U S ?

Which letter should replace the question mark to continue the series?

25. If $4 \times 2 = 12$, then $5 \times 5 = ?$

26. What number should replace the question mark?

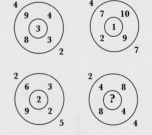

27. Place two of the four-letter groups together to make a word. The word is hyphenated.

IECE - TONE -
TWOP - LEST -
TAIL - BACS

28. Trace out a ten-letter word in any direction, using each letter once only.

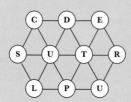

29. How many degrees are there in this angle?

(a) $128\frac{4}{7}^\circ$ (d) $141\frac{1}{7}^\circ$

(b) $130\frac{1}{7}^\circ$ (e) $146\frac{3}{7}^\circ$

(c) $133\frac{3}{7}^\circ$

30. Which circle is most like E?

Is it A, B, C, or D?

E

A   B   C   D

31. A word can be placed in the parentheses that has the same meaning as the words outside. What is it?

BIRD (_ _ _ _ _ _) GRUMBLE

32. Starting at an outside square and moving in any direction, spell out the name of a bird.

AR	PA	BU
IG	DG	RR
ER	US	IT

33. Place a word in the parentheses that when placed on the end of the first word makes a word, and when placed in front of the second word also makes a word.

BUTTER (_ _ _) FISHING

34. What number should replace the question mark?

26	38	70	22	10
41	26	38	70	?
17	41	26	38	70
6	17	41	26	38

35. If the missing letters in the circle are correctly inserted they will form an eight-letter word. The word does not have to be read in a clockwise direction, but the letters are consecutive. What is the word and missing letters?

36. Find a one-word anagram for PEAS PAUL.

37. What fraction should replace the question mark?

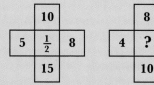

38. Which word means the fear of glass?

(a) NEOPHOBIA
(b) NELOPHOBIA
(c) DORAPHOBIA
(d) LOGOPHOBIA
(e) NECROPHOBIA

39. Find a twelve-letter nautical term made up from two six-letter words—one inside the star, one outside.

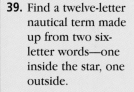

40. What temperature below is 104° Fahrenheit changed to Celsius?

(a) 34°C
(b) 36°C
(c) 38°C
(d) 40°C
(e) 42°C

TEST 17

1. What same three-letter word when inserted into the following letter combinations will make four new words? The word to be inserted must not be split, and the order of the letter combinations must not be changed. For example: The word AND inserted into the letter combination HY makes HANDY.

   ST   ARE   CHIE   SNER

2. What number should replace the question mark?

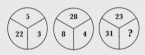

3. Which is the odd one out?

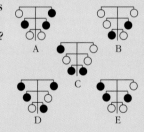

4. Which is the odd one out?

   Arcadia, Utopia, Atlantis, Avalon, Shangri-La

5. Insert the name of an animal into the bottom line to complete the three-letter words.

A	A	L	G	R	Y	P	O
R	S	E	A	A	O	E	A

6. Solve the cryptogram below. Each letter has been substituted with a different letter of the alphabet.

   KM DWRVNVCR RSVMZC
   RSVC VC RSL GLCR DB
   KJJ FDXJEC. K WLCCVPVCR
   BLKXC RSL CKPL RD GL
   RXTL. —EDTY JKXCDM

7. Insert a word that can be tacked on to the first word and placed in front of the second to form two different words.

OUT		WAY

8. Moving clockwise, take one letter from each circle to spell out an eight-letter word meaning "complex." You have to find the starting point.

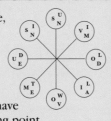

9. Which is the missing section?

A   B   C

10. Change one letter in each word to produce a well-known phrase.

FIT OF KISS

11.

2	6	9	4	7	8	1
4	1	8	2	3	9	6
9	3	7	6	1	4	2
8	7	3	?	?	2	4
7	8	1	?	?	6	9
3	9	6	7	4	1	8
1	4	2	8	9	3	7

Which four numbers below should replace the question marks?

6	1
3	2

6	1
2	3

2	1
6	3

A   B   C

1	6
3	2

1	2
3	6

D   E

12. Spiral clockwise around the perimeter and finish at the center square to spell out a nine-letter word. The word starts at one of the corner squares. You have to provide the missing letter.

R	A	V
B	E	E
E	T	

13. Decipher each anagram to find two phrases that are spelled differently but sound alike. For example: A NAME, AN AIM.

TAUGHT HOST
TUFT SHAFT

14. I am causing an unctuous liquid to flow in contact with agitated bodies of a compound formed by portions of hydrogen and oxygen. What am I doing?

15. Taking the respective numerical position of letters in the alphabet, decode the following: 1183452018915131685

For example: LITTLE GIANT = 12, 9, 20, 20, 12, 5, 7, 9, 1, 14, 20 or 12920201257911420.

16. Each large square contains the letters of a nine-letter word. Find the two words, which are synonyms.

	U	T	D
A	N	A	P	R
O	I	R	E	E
V	I	T		

17. Bill and Al share a certain sum of money in the ratio 5:4 and Al ends up with $60. How much money was shared?

18. Complete the five words so that two letters are common to each word. That is, the same two letters that end the first word also start the second word, and so on. The two letters that end the fifth word are the first two letters of the first word, thus completing the pattern.

_ _ O R _ _
_ _ E F _ _
_ _ L A _ _
_ _ N I _ _
_ _ L U _ _

19. Underline the two words inside the parentheses that the word outside the parentheses always has.

VOLCANO
(SMOKE,
ROCK,
FUMES,
WATER,
CRATER)

20. What number should replace the question mark?

100 $96\frac{1}{2}$ $89\frac{1}{2}$? 65 $47\frac{1}{2}$ $26\frac{1}{2}$

21. Alter one letter in each word below to reveal a familiar phrase:

SOME GAS GOT GUILT AN I SAY

22. Moving through the doorways spell out an eight-letter word.

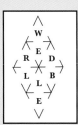

23. Simplify $\frac{825}{900}$ as a fraction.

24. Which word means the same as HAPLESS?

(a) THREATENING
(b) UNFORTUNATE
(c) VAPID
(d) CAPRICIOUS
(e) OBTUSE

25. How many squares are there in this diagram?

26. Rearrange the two five-letter words to form a ten-letter word meaning "advanced fortification."

RABID HEDGE

27. Find the entire word that contains these middle letters.

_ _ _ NKYD _ _

28. Fill in the missing letters for the name of a group of animals.

_ E _ A _ E _ I _

29. Find a six-letter word made up of only the following four letters.

M G O N

30. Which is the odd one out?

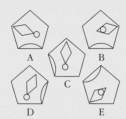

31. Fill in the missing letters to complete the word.

_ _ G E W _ _ _

32. Place the letters in the grid to make a tree and a donkey.

ABBCOORRU

33. You have 60 cube blocks. What is the minimum number that have to be taken away in order to leave a solid cube?

(a) 27   (d) 33

(b) 29   (e) 35

(c) 31

34. If the missing letters in the two circles below are correctly inserted they will form synonymous words. The words do not have to be read in a clockwise direction, but the letters are consecutive. What are the words and missing letters?

35. Complete these musical terms.

B	U		S
A			A
S	A		E

36. What is the mathematical sign for factorial?

(a) !

(b) ≈

(c) »

(d) /–

(e) M==

37. Starting from a corner square and continuing in a spiral to the center, fill in the missing letters to make a nine-letter word.

O	S	
	E	I
U	T	D

38. Which circle's letters cannot be arranged into a six-letter word?

A   B   C   D

39.

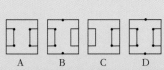

If ⊃C is to ( ) then ⊥⊥ is to:

A   B   C   D

40. What is kept in a BINNACLE?

(a) SAIL
(b) FLAG
(c) BALLAST
(d) COMPASS
(e) CUTLERY

TEST 18

1. To which of the four boxes at right can a dot be added so that it then meets the same conditions as in the box to the left?

A   B   C   D

2. What number should replace the question mark?

17 8 $12\frac{3}{4}$ $11\frac{1}{8}$ $8\frac{1}{2}$ $14\frac{1}{4}$?

3. Move horizontally and vertically, but not diagonally, to spell out a twelve-letter word. You have to find the starting point and provide the missing letters.

E			A
R	I	C	R
E	T	C	A

4. IMPRISON : JAIL

EXILE :
      PUNISH
      COUNTRY
      DEPART
      BANISH
      ERADICATE

5. Change one letter only in each word and then rearrange the five new words to form a well-known phrase.

NOW I BURN LEAD OVEN

6. What letter should replace the question mark?

7. Each number has a choice of three letters. Dial an inventor (6, 4): 417945 1365

ABC **1** DEF **2** GHI **3**
JKL **4** MNO **5** PQR **6**
STU **7** VWX **8** YZ **9**
* **0** **#**

8. Add one letter, not necessarily the same letter, to the front, end, or middle of each word to find two words that are similar in meaning.

RUSH GRIN

9.  is to as

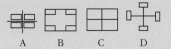 is to:

A   B   C   D

10. The white dot moves counter-clockwise one corner at each stage and the black dot moves counterclockwise three corners at each stage. In how many stages will they be together in the same corner?

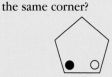

11. Which word in the right-hand column can be added to the list in the left-hand column?

BEAM	FIX
DOWN	SET
RISE	MOVE
SCREEN	HOLD
DRY	TIE

12. Solve the cryptic clue below. The answer is a ten-letter anagram contained within the clue.

> FLIPPANT JIBE
> MADE BY A
> SICK CREW

13. Insert the eight four-figure numbers in the grid, four reading across and four reading down.

4169
3613
1735
2975
7832
8127
6217
7461

14. Which number is the odd one out?

15. Eliminate twelve letters from the phrase below to leave a seven-letter word meaning "component."

GENTLEMEN'S AGREEMENT

16. What is the average of the numbers on the reverse side of these dice?

17. Eight square pieces of paper, all exactly the same size, have been placed on top of each other so that some part of each piece of paper can be seen. Sheet H is completely shown and was, therefore, the last piece of paper to be placed. Which was the first piece of paper to be placed? Can this fact be determined?

```
+---+---+---+
| G | C | D |
+---+---+   |
| B | H |   |
|   |   +---+
|   |   | F |
+---+---+   |
| A | E |   |
+---+---+---+
```

18. Change one letter in each word below to get three words that are members of the same category. For example: FOUL, SAX, TIN = FOUR, SIX, TEN.

BEAT, SHOP, RANT

19. Fill in the blanks to form building terms.

_ E _ S _ H _ L _
_ H _ E _ H _ L _
_ E _ E _ E _ T _

20. Solve the anagram to find the name of a famous person to complete the clerihew.

"FIRED MUD SNUG"

Said _____ _____,
"I'm really annoyed!
There wasn't a theme,
To my latest dream."

21. What is the product of the smallest prime number multiplied by the largest odd number?

17	71	4
11	67	19
37	87	97

22. Make up four pairs of words and find the odd one.

MONEY	SALAD	PENNY
MILK	BELT	POSY
PINCHING	DAYS	BUTTER

23. Going down each row, take one letter from each word to spell out an American city. Then do the same again, this time using different letters to spell out another American city. Then do the same again to find a third American city.

E	M	E	N	D	A	T	E
D	O	N	A	T	I	O	N
B	L	U	E	C	A	P	S
H	E	A	R	T	I	L	Y
H	A	L	L	M	A	R	K
S	A	U	C	I	E	S	T

24. Which two words are similar in meaning?

DOGGER
HOUND
FALSEHOOD
FISHING VESSEL
JARGON
STEADFAST

25. Which hexagon is most like E? Is it A, B, C, or D?

E

A

B

C

D

26. Which of these is not an anagram of a soldier?

(a) ZARINAJ
(b) SSCHEURA
(c) BATMURO
(d) EERETLUM
(e) LENTINES
(f) NAMLEGFU

27. Fill in the missing number that will fit the rule or rules of the example below.

3	1	6	17
5	4	8	19
7	9	10	?
9	16	12	29

28. What is the meaning of PARANG?

    (a) BEEF STEW
    (b) BALCONY
    (c) WAGON
    (d) KNIFE
    (e) LAKE

29. What is the name given to a group of SEAFOWL?

    (a) DOPPING
    (b) FLUSH
    (c) CLOUD
    (d) FLOCK
    (e) GAME
    (f) DULE

30. Starting at an outside square and moving in any direction, spell out the name of an insect.

BO	BE	ET
TT	UE	LI
LE	NE	BL

31. Which diagram has most in common with diagram E?

E

A

B

C

D

32. Which of the following is always associated with ISTHMUS?

    (a) ICE FLOES
    (b) MOUNTAINS
    (c) RAVINES
    (d) LAND
    (e) CLIFFS

33. What value should be placed at D to balance the 10-unit-long scale?

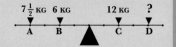

$7\frac{1}{2}$ KG   6 KG   12 KG ?
A   B   C   D

34. Which word can be placed on the end of these words to make new words?

OF
HAS
BIT (_ _ _)
BAT
ROT

35. Find a six-letter word made up of only the following four letters.

LCFE

36. What number should replace the question mark?

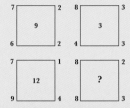

37. Simplify to find x:

$$\frac{3 - (4 \times 3)}{(4 \times 3) - 7} = x$$

38. What number will replace the question mark?

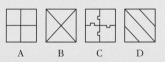

39. Make one word using all ten letters of these two words:

LOATH CARED

Clue: *Has eight plane faces*

40. Which is the odd one out?

A   B   C   D

TEST 19

1. 478531978447892

Multiply by five the number of even numbers that are immediately followed by an odd number in the series above. What is the answer?

2. What word is opposite in meaning to OPULENT?

BLEAK, DESTITUTE, GENTLE, THIN, UNIFORM

3. What four-letter word can be placed at the end of each of these letters to form six new words?

SH
T
D   (_ _ _ _)
TH
F
G

7. Unscramble these four anagrammed words to determine their commonality or relationship:

ANTRUM
TRACER
RECIPE
DOMAINS

4. Which is the missing square?

A   B   C   D

8. Four of these words share a common feature. Which of the words does not have this common feature?

WAYLAY
DISMISS
FURTHER
REFEREE
BACKPACK

5. PSEUDO (ATONE) TARTAN

Using the same rules as in the example above, what word should be in the parentheses below?

GOSPEL (_ _ _ _ _) IMPOSE

6. Which is the missing segment?

A   B   C   D

112 ❖ **TEST 19**

9. Insert the letters provided into each quadrant to form two words of a phrase—one reading clockwise around the inner circle and one clockwise around the outer circle.

NE: DIXA
SE: TEAR
SW: IOTC
NW: INNT

10. 376 : 27
984 : 76

Which two numbers below have the same relationship as the two examples above?
A. 756 : 83
B. 654 : 46
C. 822 : 14
D. 691 : 15
E. 532 : 17

11. On the last day of a 7-day trip, a backpacker walks 22 miles, which raises the average distance he has walked each day from 15 miles to 16 miles. How far would he have had to walk on the last day to bring his average mileage per day to 18?

12. What number should replace the question mark?

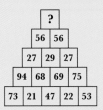

13. Add one letter, not necessarily the same letter, to each of these two words to make them synonymous:

BEAK RUSH

14. Insert two letters in each pair of parentheses that will finish the first word and start the second. Reading the inserted pairs of letters downwards will spell out a six-letter word that is sometimes said to create an opening.

CA (_ _) ED
VI (_ _) KE
HO (_ _) AN

15. Insert these consonants to form a magic square where all five words read the same across and down.

GDDRB
TGDTN
DSDD

	A		E	
A		I		E
	I			E
E			E	
	E	E		

16. The seven horses are positioned in the stalls ready for the start of the race. In how many different possible ways can the first three places be filled?

SIR BARTON
GALLANT FOX
OMAHA
WAR ADMIRAL
WHIRLAWAY
COUNT FLEET
ASSAULT

17. What do these words have in common?

UNCLOAKING, DISHWASHER, CROSSFIRE, DOPINESS

18. Insert a word in the parentheses that means the same as the definitions outside the parentheses.

BLACK ( ) FOUNTAIN

19. FACTORY, AGILITY, ATHEISM, SEMINAR

What comes next in this sequence?

ABDOMEN, KILLJOY, CONVICT, CONNIVE, BEESWAX

20. What phrase can be inserted into the far-right line in order to complete the eight three-letter words read left to right?

T	I	
R	■	
I	N	
C	O	
K	■	
O	D	
R	■	
T	E	
R	I	
E	V	
A	I	
T	■	

21. Find the eight-letter word.

(1 2 3 4) M I S T – H O U R (5 6 7 8)
(5 7 1 6) _ _ _ _ _ _ _ _ (8 2 3 4)

22. What number should replace the question mark?

7 12 8¼ 10¾ 9½ 9½ ?

23. BULLDOG, HOLIDAY, FRANCHISE, ITALICS, ?

Which word below completes the sequence?

SWEETMEATS, DISGRACE, POSTAGE, GRACIOUS

24. Place two of the three-letter groups together to make a poem.

RHY - TON - NAR - NET - MUS - ARI - HYM - SON

25. Which temperature below is 25° Celsius changed to Fahrenheit?

(a) 73°F (d) 79°F
(b) 75°F (e) 81°F
(c) 77°F

26. Which word will fit in front of these words to form new words?

(_ _ _ _)

LET
LING
LIGHT
LIT
DUST

27. Fill in the blank spaces to find astronomical terms.

_ E _ E _ R _ T _
_ U _ E _ N _ V _
_ A _ E _ L _ T _

28. Rearrange the letters to form two seven-letter words that are synonyms.

Each word commences with the central letter.

29. Group pairs of letters to form four four-letter tools; one pair is not used.

RK	JA	FI
LE	SP	AD
ZE	CK	FO

30.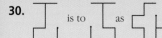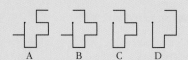

A   B   C   D

31. What is the product of the largest odd number multiplied by the smallest cubed number?

101	111	37
93	71	32
64	63	27

32. What is the meaning of LIBRETTO?

(a) TRAVELING LIBRARY
(b) BOOK OF ANECDOTES
(c) WORDS OF AN OPERA
(d) PLAY SOFTLY
(e) PLAY FASTER

33. Which word means the same as HEINOUS?

(a) INIQUITOUS
(b) ABLE
(c) SPECIAL
(d) FULSOME
(e) HAZY

34. Place three of the two-letter groups together to form a boat.

SE - SA - CR - AN - MP - UI

35. Following the rule of the first example, fill in the missing word inside the parentheses.

GAME (MAGI) AVID
2   1   1234 3 4

LOPE (_ _ _ _) OMEN
2 1   1 2 3 4   3 4

36. Which is the odd one out?

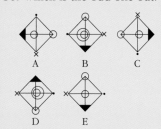

A   B   C

D   E

37. Find a one-word anagram from the two words below.

TASTE CANS

38. ARM is to RADIUS as LEG is to:

(a) PHALANGES
(b) FIBULA
(c) LUMBAR
(d) THORACIC
(e) PELVIS

39. What number should replace the question mark?

$12 + 6 \div 2 + 1 \times 5 + 6 = ?$

40. Which number is the odd one out?

4932, 4376, 6516, 2952, 8136

TEST 20

1. Which of the five boxes below has most in common with the box at right?

A B C D

3. 19 : 132 : 923
Which set has the same relationship as the above?

(a) 25 : 174 : 1217
(b) 18 : 34 : 66
(c) 23 : 161 : 1127
(d) 12 : 73 : 433
(e) 2 : 18 : 54

2. Which three-letter word, when inserted into the following letter combinations, will form four new words? The word to be inserted must not be split and the order of the letter combination must not be changed. For example, the word AND inserted into the letter combination CY makes CANDY.

WON CD REML MRN

4. ERCTA : REACT

ALERT :

TRALE
ALTER
LATER
RATEL
TALER

5. If 9L of a C = 9 lives of a cat, can you decode the following?

9P in the SS

6. Change TABLE to SALT by following these instructions:

	TABLE
Change a letter:	_ _ _ _ _
Remove a letter:	_ _ _ _
Change a letter:	SALT

7. How many more circles of the same size as the one already placed will completely cover the hexagon?

8. What number should replace the question mark?

9. Which clock face is the odd one out?

A   B   C   D

10. Insert the missing word in the crossword.

11. Place a word in the parentheses that will finish the first word and start the second.

ARC (_ _ _) RING

12. Decipher each anagram to find two phrases that are spelled differently but sound alike. For example:
A NAME, AN AIM.
CANNON WOKE   NOT ONION

13. Which of the following continues the sequence?

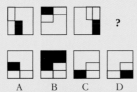

?

A B C D

14. Each pair of words by association leads to another word. Fill in the missing words.

TIP
PLAY } OFF

HEAD
SAFETY } A) _____

SHOW
SUN } B) _____

TOUCH
STEREO } TYPE

HAND

C) _____

OUT

15. Put the words into the correct order and then say whether the statement formed is true or false.

OF ETYMOLOGY CALLED STUDY THE INSECTS IS

16. Out of 100 women surveyed leaving Macy's, 70 had purchased perfume, 83 had purchased cosmetics, 58 had purchased shoes, and 98 had purchased an item of clothing. How many must have purchased all four items?

17. What five-letter word inserted downwards completes the five different four-letter words starting BAR?

BAR (_)
BAR (_)
BAR (_)
BAR (_)
BAR (_)

18. SINGLE is to ONE as CIPHER is to

HUNDRED
TEN
FIVE
TWO
ZERO

19. Which two of these words are opposite in meaning?

FAINT, WEAK, LARGE, STURDY, GREAT, SERIOUS

20.

Which option continues the above sequence?

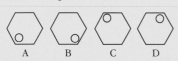

A   B   C   D

21. Rearrange the two five-letter words to form a ten-letter word meaning "good eater."

ROAST GNOME

22. What number should replace the question mark?

8		2
	102	
7		10

9		3
	152	
6		10

7		3
	136	
7		11

7		7
	?	
7		21

23. What is the meteorological symbol for cold front?

(a) ▲▼▲

(b) ▲▲▲

(c) ◠◠

(d) ○

(e) ☀

24. Here is a list of fish. Which fish from List B should fit into List A to follow a scheme?

A	B
?	HERRING
REMORA	WRASSE
ANGEL	BLOATER
SALMON	SARDINE
SHRIMP	
EEL	

25. Which diagram has the most in common with the diagram marked E?

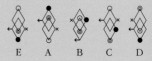

E   A   B   C   D

26. Simplify $\dfrac{2}{9} \div \dfrac{7}{18}$.

27. Which of these is not an island?

(a) PUFFIN
(b) MORELLO
(c) CAYMAN
(d) TAHITI
(e) BAHAMAS
(f) TIMOR

28. What is the meaning of PANACHE?

(a) DISMAY
(b) TRUST
(c) SWAGGER
(d) MEDICINE
(e) MISERY

29. Place four of the three-letter groups together to make two six-letter words.

SHE – HAY – DEL – CLA – LVE –
VIT – VIC – RIC

30. Which is the astronomical symbol for Venus?

(a) ☿
(b) ♀
(c) ♂
(d) ♃
(e) ○

31. What is the product of the lowest even number multiplied by the highest square number? For example: Square numbers are $4 \times 4 = 16$, $7 \times 7 = 49$, etc.

63	64	121
89	56	97
10	8	19

32. Which diagram has the most in common with D?

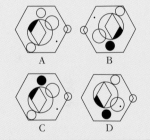

A   B

C   D

33. Find three insects hidden in the following sentence: "Pecan trees and beech trees have leaves parallel to the ground."

34. How many degrees are there in this angle?

(a) 125°
(b) 130°
(c) 140°
(d) 144°
(e) 150°

35. What is the S.I. metric prefix for DECA (10^{-6})?

(a) D   (d) DA
(b) da   (e) de
(c) d

36. What is the opposite of SOMNOLENT?

(a) EXTREME
(b) OFFENDED
(c) ORIGINAL
(d) SAGGING
(e) WAKEFUL

37. If the missing letters in the two circles are correctly inserted, they will form synonyms. The words do not have to be read in a clockwise direction, but the letters are consecutive. What are the words and missing letters?

38. What would you be wearing if you wore a GLENGARRY?

(a) A CAP
(b) A DRESS
(c) SHOES
(d) A HALTER
(e) A COAT

39. The vowels have been omitted from this quotation. Can you replace them?

THRHSDDRMWTCHHSSTPPD

40. What number should replace the question mark?

TEST 21

1. Change a letter in each word to find a phrase.

CUE I CATER

2. Jim, Sid, Alf, Jack, and George were members of the same bowling team. Jack scored more than Alf, Sid scored more than Jack, Alf scored more than Jim, and George scored less than Sid. Which one of the following conclusions is, therefore, proved to be true?

A. Jack scored more than Jim but less than Alf.

B. Jack scored less than Jim and Sid.

C. Jack outscored Jim by more than he outscored Alf.

D. George scored more than Alf.

E. None of the above conclusions is proved to be true.

3. Going clockwise, take one letter from each circle and spell out an eight-letter word meaning "overjoyed." You have to find the starting point.

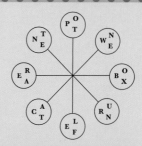

4. Solve the clues to find two six-letter words.

A. Tiny

B. Painter or sculptor

5. Solve the next three clues to find three four-letter words that use exactly the same twelve letters as in the two solutions to 4.

C. Thin fog

D. Rip apart

E. Subdivision of a military formation

6. Complete the palindrome below:

_ _ M _ _ _ N _ _ T _ _ _ R _ _ _ I _ _ _ E _ _ _ _

Clue: *Males translate notes*

---

7. I am projecting circumspection in the direction of a natural current of air. What am I doing?

---

8. Taking the respective numerical position of letters in the alphabet, decode the following:

1618913141514141

For example: LITTLE GIANT = 12, 9, 20, 20, 12, 5, 7, 9, 1, 14, 20, or 12920201257911420.

---

9. What number should replace the question mark?

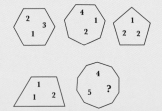

---

10. Find the logic behind this pattern of numbers and complete the four missing numbers in the top right-hand corner.

7	4	9	6		
3	6	9	4		
6	3	7	4	9	6
9	4	7	3	6	9
4	9	6	3	7	4
7	3	6	9	4	7

---

11. Which word will carry on the sequence?

BABBLE, EMBOSS, SHEKEL, LOVING, GUIDER, RINGED, ?

(a) CHUBBY   (b) GUILTY
(c) HOURLY   (d) HINGED
(e) DIVEST   (f) IMPUGN

---

12. Each larger square contains the letters of a nine-letter word.

S	T	E		
A	L	I	Z	Q
P	K	C	A	Z
		U	L	I

Find the two nine-letter words that are synonyms.

13. Change one letter in each word to get three words that are members of the same category. For example: FOUL, SAX, TIN = FOUR, SIX, TEN

LIMB, PARK, SEAL

18. Which is the odd one out?

A B C D

14. Make up four pairs of words and find the odd one.

GAMES	POTATO	TENNIS
LAUGHING	WAR	DIZZY
SALAD	MATCH	HYENA

19. NEDRA, ELLEN, FLORA, NOEL, DENNIS, ROLF, TINA, EDNA, ANITA, NELL, LEON, AND ARDEN SINNED.

Put all the names into a different order so that all of the above paragraph becomes palindromic.

15. In the array of numbers at right, what is the difference between the highest square number and the square of the lowest prime number?

15	4	21	12	7	14
11	8	36	27	25	32
17	10	23	18	6	55
44	16	19	9	13	38

16. Spiral clockwise around the perimeter squares and finish at the center square to spell out a nine-letter word. The word starts at one of the corner squares. You must provide the missing letters.

G	O	N
	L	
T		O

17. Insert the letters of the phrase below into the grid to find two related words.

SPECTRUM PLANER
Clue: *Database*

20. How many triangles appear in this figure?

23. Place two of the four-letter groups together to make a word.

CIAL - PACI - OFFI - FISE - WARS - OUT

21. If you fold this piece of card along the lines to form a regular solid (all surfaces of equal size), what will its name be?

(a) TETRAHEDRON
(b) HEXAHEDRON
(c) OCTAHEDRON
(d) DODECAHEDRON
(e) ICOSAHEDRON

24. Place the letters in the grid to form a flower and a bird.

A C I L N N O P U

25. What is the name given to a group of peacocks?

(a) MESS
(b) MUSTER
(c) SHOWER
(d) SHOW
(e) NYE
(f) NIDE

22. Complete the grid with the letters provided so that all the words have a common theme.

T Y A
C N P
L S K
M G

	A	
	I	
	A	
	S	

26. Starting from a corner square and continuing in a counter-clockwise spiral to the center, fill in the missing letters to make a nine-letter word.

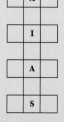

	U	L
T	Y	O
A	R	

27. In how many ways can the word "CUBE" be read? Start at the central letter "C" and move in any direction.

```
      E
    E B E
  E B U B E
E B U C U B E
  E B U B E
    E B U
      E
```

28. Which temperature is 86° Fahrenheit changed to Celsius?

(a) 30°C
(b) 32°C
(c) 34°C
(d) 36°C
(e) 38°C

29. Make one word using all of these ten letters:

BIRTH COINS
Clue: *An illness*

30. What is the product of the smallest odd number multiplied by the largest cube number? For example: $4 \times 4 \times 4 = 64$, a cube number.

216	177	15
204	9	404
99	17	11

31. Change this fraction to a decimal.

$$\frac{5}{8} =$$

32. Find pairs of letters to form four four-letter boats; one pair is not used.

DH	IG	BA
HU	OW	SC
OW	LK	BR

33. If the missing letters in the circle below are correctly inserted they will form an eight-letter word. The word does not have to be read in a clockwise direction, but the letters are consecutive. What is the word and missing letters?

34. Find the eight-letter word that follows the example's pattern.

(1 2 3 4) S I C K - F O R D (5 6 7 8)
(8 2 1 5) _ _ _ _ _ _ _ _ (7 6 3 4)

35. Moving in any direction, trace out a ten-letter word, using each letter once only.

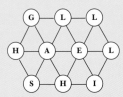

36. Which is the odd one out?

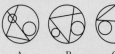

37. If 9 × 9 = 74,
then 7 × 2 = ?

38. Fill in the missing letters to complete the word.

_ _ _ _ _ _ U R T _ _

39. A stone is dropped over the edge of a cliff. After 5 seconds, how far has it fallen?

(a) 380 ft.
(b) 400 ft.
(c) 420 ft.
(d) 440 ft.
(e) 460 ft.

40. Which of these anagrams is not a strong wind?

(a) SONMOON
(b) QLULSA
(c) TKKIIBA
(d) NORTODA
(e) HYRZPE
(f) CROCSIO

TEST 22

1. Find the starting point and track from letter to letter along the lines to spell out an eighteen-letter word.

2. SCIENCE (CICERO) HISTORY

Using the same rules as in the example above, what word should appear in the parentheses below?

TOURIST (_ _ _ _ _ _) SCOLDED

3. What number should replace the question mark?

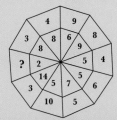

4.

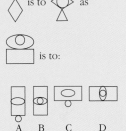

5. Arrange these twelve words into four ten-letter words using three small words for each ten-letter word. For example: The words MOST, HER, HIT could be arranged to form the ten-letter word HITHERMOST.

AGE, ANT, END, DISC, HABIT, IN, OR, OR, OUR, PRESS, SABLE, SUP

6. What letter should replace the question mark?

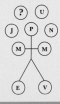

7. Solve the three anagrams to produce a well-known saying.

_ _ _ _ _ _ _ _ _ _ _ _ _ _ _ _ _

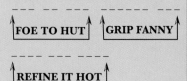

↑**FOE TO HUT**↑   ↑**GRIP FANNY**↑

_ _ _ _ _ _ _ _ _ _ _

↑**REFINE IT HOT**↑

8. Choose one word from the right-hand column to put with the words in the left-hand column.

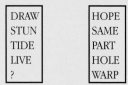

DRAW	HOPE
STUN	SAME
TIDE	PART
LIVE	HOLE
?	WARP

9. Complete the palindrome below:

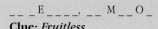

_ _ _ E _ _ _ _, _ _ M _ _ O _
Clue: _Fruitless_

10. I take a certain journey and travel the first half of the complete distance at a speed of 20 mph. How fast would I have to travel over the second half of the journey to average a speed of 40 mph for the whole journey?

11. How many triangles appear in this figure?

12. Eliminate thirteen letters from the phrase below to leave a word meaning "examine cursorily."

FOR BETTER OR FOR WORSE

13. Ten numbers (1–10) were put in a bag and one number drawn out. Two of six people predicted the correct number by making the following statements prior to the number being drawn out. Which number was drawn out?

Alan: It was an odd number.
Bill: It was a square number (1, 4, or 9).
Connie: It was a number less than 7.
David: It was a prime number (2, 3, 5, or 7).
Eileen: It was an even number.
Fiona: It was between 3 and 7 inclusive.

14. The vowels have been removed from a well-known phrase and the remaining letters have been arranged in groups of four. What is the phrase?

NWBR MSSW PCLN

15. What number should replace the question mark?

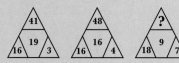

16. Change MONDAY to THURSDAY. The asterisks in each word are common to the word above it.

MONDAY

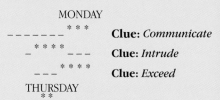

        * * *   **Clue:** *Communicate*

_ _ _ _ _ _ _

   * * * *   **Clue:** *Intrude*

_   _ _ _

      * * * *   **Clue:** *Exceed*

_ _ _

THURSDAY

  * *

17. If meat in a river (3 in 6) is T(HAM)ES, can you find a composer's name in lights (6 in 9)?

18. Which comes next?

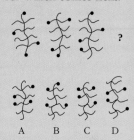

?

A   B   C   D

19. Find the three reptiles hidden in the following sentence: "To avoid decay, man has priorities: to advise caution in all activities."

20. Complete the words below, which are all synonyms.

O _ _ _ A _ _ E
_ A _ _ I E _
_ U _ _ _ E
_ I _ _ _ A _ _ E

Clue: *Stumbling block*

21. Supply the missing words inside the parentheses. Each word must logically follow the word above it and precede the word below it. For example: BALL (PARK) LAND.

SIDE

(_ _ _ _)

DOWN

(_ _ _ _)

TAIL

(_ _ _ _)

POST

(_ _ _ _)

LINE

22. Which word means the fear of SLEEP?

(a) OIKOPHOBIA
(b) PANPHOBIA
(c) POLYPHOBIA
(d) HYPNOPHOBIA
(e) CROMOPHOBIA

23. Rearrange the letters in each circle to find two seven-letter words that are synonyms.

Each word commences with the central letter.

24. What number replaces the question mark?

1   9   36   ?   225   441   784

25. Which symbol continues the sequence?

A   B   C   D

26. Complete the sequence.

$\frac{1}{4}$ $\frac{3}{4}$ $2\frac{1}{4}$?

K   N   R   ?

27. Place three of the two-letter groups together to form an insect.

BE - ET - LA - TA - SE - TS

28. Which is the odd one out in each circle?

Circle 1: 972 363 176 781 594 792

Circle 2: 176 385 462 671 791 891

29. Which two words are similar in meaning?

PORRINGER, DISH, DECANTER, HAIR NET, STRAINER, BASKET

30. Which of the following is associated with LUX?

(a) FIREWORKS   (d) BRIDGES
(b) ILLUMINATION   (e) CANALS
(c) FOUNTAINS

31. Starting at an outside square and moving in any direction, spell out the name of a bird.

IN	DW	ER
CU	CK	DA
PE	OD	WO

32. Which symbol replaces the question mark?

A   B   C   D   E

33. What is a DUODECIMAL a system of?

(a) FOURS   (d) TWELVES
(b) SIXTEENS   (e) TENS
(c) EIGHTS

34. Fill in the blanks to find boys' names.

A		R		N
W				G
N		I		L

35. What number should replace the question mark?

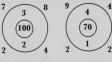

36. A word can be placed in the parentheses that has the same meaning as the words outside. What is it?

CONCEAL (_ _ _ _) SKIN

37. What number should replace the question mark?

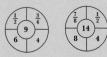

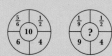

38. Which two words have opposite meanings?

LURID, PLUMP, SECONDARY, MEAGER, CABALISTIC, DAUNTLESS

39. Which circle's letters cannot be arranged into a six-letter word?

A   B   C   D

40. Complete these names of tools.

A		V		L
G				V
R		Z		R

TEST 23

1. What two letters are missing from the last box?

MA	DE
AP	TE

CA	CI
PR	NA

RO	MA
AI	CI

NI	TE
SE	?

2. Insert the word that finishes the first word and starts the second.

HAS		ACE

3. Match each word in column A with a word in column B.

A	B
BROWN	SAPPHIRE
BLACK	JADE
BLUE	SABLE
GREEN	UMBER

4.

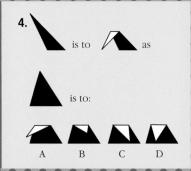

A B C D

5. TURMOIL is to TROUBLE as TRAGEDY is to:

SOMBER, DISASTER, PITY, DRAMA, EARTHQUAKE

6. Arrange the letters below to find two words.

NTEGOMYDBA

Clue: *Personal attraction*

7. What two letters, when placed in the square, will construct ten four-letter words by using each of the letters in the first circle once to start the words and each of the letters in the second circle once to complete them?

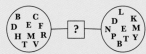

8. What is the product of the second-highest odd number in the left grid multiplied by the second-lowest even number in the right grid?

9	11	2	28
46	3	15	52
36	9	8	26
13	27	10	7

12	2	42	25
3	9	16	15
18	8	29	11
12	7	31	10

9. Each large square contains the letters of a nine-letter word. Find the two words that are synonyms.

R	V	N	
I	E	T	N	E
A	R	A	M	S
	T	T	E

10. Which one of the following is not an anagram of KNICKERBOCKER GLORY?

(a) KICK GROCER BROKENLY
(b) BEG KINKY CLOCK ERROR
(c) GREY LONER KICK BRICK
(d) KEY BORING CORK CLERK
(e) ROCKY GIRL BROKE NECK
(f) CLERK COOK KING BERRY
(g) REBLOCK KINKY GROCER

11. There are five stations from A to B. How many different single tickets must be printed so that it is possible to buy a ticket from any station to any other?

12. The height of the Eiffel Tower is 150 meters plus half its own height. How high is the Eiffel Tower?

13. What comes next in the below sequence?

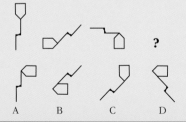

14. Taking the respective position of letters in the alphabet, decode the following:

21141141191612920
For example: LITTLE GIANT = 12, 9, 20, 20, 12, 5, 7, 9, 1, 14, 20, or 12920201257911420.

15. Complete the five words so that two letters are common to each word. That is, the same two letters that end the first word also start the second word, and so on. The two letters that end the fifth word are the first two letters of the first word, thus completing the pattern.

_ _ A Z _ _
_ _ R U _ _
_ _ E A _ _
_ _ I R _ _
_ _ R E _ _

16. How many more circles of the same size as the one already placed on the square will completely cover it?

17. Find the eight-letter word.

(1 2 3 4) DOVE – PAIR (5 6 7 8)
(2 3 4 8) _ _ _ _ _ _ _ _ (5 6 7 1)

18. Work horizontally and vertically from square to square to spell out a twelve-letter word. You must find the starting point and provide the missing letters.

	A	T	A
I	T		E
N		B	R

19. Pair the words below to form four hyphenated words. Use each word only once.

DOUBLE	SPOT
SECTION	CROSS
CHECK	DEALER
DOWN	BOW

20. Each number stands for a choice of three letters. Decode the following to dial a famous classical composer (6, 6):
377718513426

ABC 1	DEF 2	GHI 3
JKL 4	MNO 5	PQR 6
STU 7	VWX 8	YZ 9
*	0	#

21. Insert the letters provided into each quadrant to form two words that form a phrase, one reading clockwise around the inner circle and one reading counterclockwise around the outer circle.

NE : NEIL
SE : DANT
SW : NETT
NW : ICMY

22. What number should replace the question mark?

$7 - 2 \times 6 + 8 \div 2 + 3 = ?$

23. What number should be next in this sequence?

4 6 6 2 4 2 4 ?

24. Place two of the three-letter groups together to make a bird.

GON - VER - WID - PLO - SPA - KLE - ROR - DUC

25. Place two four-letter groups together to make an eight-letter word that means "sky blue":

LEAN - TURE - CERU - PAST - UOSE - ELLE

26. Simplify $\dfrac{350}{575}$ as a fraction.

27. Which word will fit in front of these words to form new words?

(_ _ _ _)   BOARD
WAYS
SADDLE
BURNS
CAR

28. What number should replace the question mark?

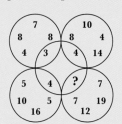

29. What is the name of the path of a shell fired into the air?

(a) HYPERBOLA
(b) PARABOLA
(c) ELLIPSOID
(d) CYCLOID

30. All of the vowels have been omitted from this quotation. See if you can replace them.

NCLRSLNGSTSBLCK

31. If $11 \times 9 = 83$, then $7 \times 7 = ?$

32. Which word belongs to this group?
CARAPACE, GARAGED, NAVIGATOR, CATAMARAN

(a) FLOTATION
(b) MURRAIN
(c) ELEVATOR
(d) DISTILLATION

36. What is the opposite of ÉCLAT?

(a) ENHANCE
(b) ILLUME
(c) CRAMPED
(d) DEMENTIA
(e) DISAPPROVAL

33. Fill in the missing letters to name a group of flowers.

_ O _ E _ A _

34. Complete these names that are associated with religion.

S		N		D
I				I
T		A		T

37. What number should replace the question mark?

38. Which of these is not a heraldic term?

(a) TREFOIL
(b) SALTIRE
(c) PALANQUIN
(d) COUCHANT
(e) SINISTER
(f) INSIGNIA

35. What number should replace the question mark?

39. If the missing letters in the circle are correctly inserted, they will form an eight-letter word. The word does not have to be read in a clockwise direction, but the letters are consecutive. What is the word and missing letters?

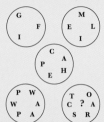

40. Which fruit comes next? Find the missing letter.

TEST 24

1. 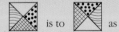 is to as

 is to:

A   B   C   D

2. Find three coins in this sentence: "The cult of the rose, new and old types, often appear new."

3. What well-known phrase appears in logical sequence in this grid?

T	E	D	N
E	S	E	E
M	H	B	K
T	O	A	M

4. 4729, 5656, 6312, ?

What comes next?

5. Solve the clues to find four six-letter words. The same three letters are represented by XYZ in each word.

X Y Z _ _ _ **Clue:** *Felt sympathy for*

_ X Y Z _ _ **Clue:** *Grudged*

_ _ X Y Z _ **Clue:** *Large deer*

_ _ _ X Y Z **Clue:** *Church platform*

6. Read clockwise to find a ten-letter word. You have to provide the missing letters. The word you are looking for starts and finishes with the same two letters.

7. Alter one letter from each word to find four new words on the same theme.

ROCK, HACK, COLT, DOME

8. From these three words, find the two words that will form an anagram that is a synonym of the word remaining. For example: LEG – MEEK – NET = MEEK – GENTLE (LEG NET)

GRADE – MAD – END

9. What shape comes next?

10. Each pair of words by association leads to another word. Fill in the missing words.

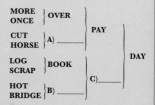

11. What number should replace the question mark?

12. LEAD MINE is an anagram of what girl's name?

13. Read clockwise around the track to find a fifteen-letter word. The overlapping letter appears twice. You must provide the missing letters.

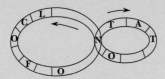

14. Find the starting point and track from letter to letter along the lines to spell out the twelve-letter name of a musical instrument.

15. Insert the same six letters into the same position to complete five seven-letter words.

_ _ A _ _ _ _   **Clue:** *Duller*
_ _ E _ _ _ _
_ _ I _ _ _ _
_ _ O _ _ _ _
_ _ U _ _ _ _   **Clue:** *Error*

16. Which pentagon should replace the question mark?

A   B   C   D   E

17. Simplify $\dfrac{4}{11} \div \dfrac{28}{22}$.

18. Solve the following clues to get two six-letter words:

(a) LAMPOON   (b) REGULAR

19. Now solve these clues to find three four-letter words that use the exact same twelve letters from the two solutions to 18.

(c) CLOSE
(d) ARRANGE
(e) CORRESPONDENCE

20. You are looking for a word in this paragraph that occurs once only. The first letter of this word is the seventh after a vowel, and this vowel is the seventh letter to appear after its last letter. What is the word?

21. If 9L of a C is 9 lives of a cat, can you decode the following?

4S in a D of C

22. Which is the odd one out?

A. ○○●○○○ B. ○○●○

C. ○●○○○ D. ○●○○○○○○

23. BRASS is an alloy made up of COPPER and which other metal?

(a) IRON   (b) TIN   (c) BRONZE   (d) NICKEL   (e) ZINC

24. What is the meaning of BLANCH?

(a) GRILL
(b) SOFTEN
(c) COOK SLOWLY
(d) WHITEN
(e) STEAM

26. How many degrees are there in this angle?

(a) 140°
(b) 145°
(c) 150°
(d) 155°
(e) 160°

25. Place four of the three-letter groups together to form two six-letter words.

MAL – ALT – IMP – MIK – LET – ADO – RES – TIN

27. Change this fraction to a decimal.

$$\frac{11}{16} =$$

28. Group pairs of letters to form four four-letter words of plants; one pair is not used.

GE	IR	BE
IS	FL	AR
AG	UM	UM

29. What number should replace the question mark?

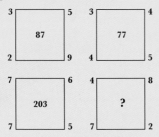

30. Make up four pairs of words and find the odd one.

FOX	CHAIN	CHIMNEY
SWEEP	MISTY	TIGER
LILY	TROT	GANG

31. Find the complete two-word noun that contains these middle letters.

_ U S T J _ _ _ _ _

32. Which is the odd one out?

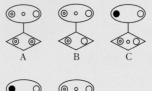

33. Place a word in the parentheses that when placed on the end of the first word makes a word and when placed in front of the second word also makes a word.

OIL (_ _ _ _) TIGHT

34. If DRINK is to LEMONADE, then FOOD is to

(a) PATELLA
(b) BANNOCK
(c) BASALT
(d) MIASMA
(e) CALYX

35. Which two words are opposite in meaning?

SECONDARY, INHERENT, VIOLATION, ACQUIRED, INSECURE, DIMINISHED

36. What word can be placed on the end of these words to form new words?

TASTE
PAIN
USE   (_ _ _ _)
COLOR
HARM

37. Which circle has the most in common with X?

X

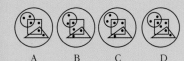

A   B   C   D

38. A word can be placed in the parentheses that has the same meaning as the words outside. What is it?

CRUDE DWELLING(_ _ _ _ _ _) SONG

39. If the missing letters in the two circles below are correctly inserted they will form synonyms. The words do not have to be read in a clockwise direction, but the letters are consecutive. What are the words and missing letters?

40. Which temperature below is 50° Celsius changed to Fahrenheit?

(a) 118°F
(b) 120°F
(c) 122°F
(d) 124°F
(e) 126°F

TEST 25

1. Find five words by starting at the top of the pyramid and taking one letter from each row. Every letter in the pyramid is used at least once.

```
        T
      E   A
    R   A   M
  S   C   P   E
S   H   D   E   O
```

2. The letters QWERTYUIOP appear only once in that order in a straight line. Can you find them? They may appear horizontally, vertically, diagonally, backwards, or forwards.

E	R	U	Y	I	O	P	Q	P	Q
T	U	Y	T	R	E	W	Q	W	O
E	Q	W	E	R	E	Y	E	I	U
T	P	O	I	Y	T	R	E	W	Q
Q	W	T	R	E	T	P	P	W	W
P	O	T	U	U	O	E	E	R	O
Y	U	I	O	I	P	R	I	I	P
I	T	P	U	O	T	Y	U	I	Y
E	R	Y	T	Y	U	T	T	U	Q
R	P	O	U	I	Y	T	R	E	W
E	E	I	E	E	E	Y	E	I	E
O	O	W	W	E	T	W	W	O	R
P	R	Q	Q	W	E	R	Q	W	T

3. Decipher each anagram to find two phrases that are spelled differently but sound alike. For example: A NAME, AN AIM.

TEAR PAGE   EGYPT ERA

4. What comes next?

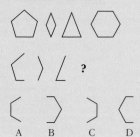

A   B   C   D

5. Fill in the missing letters and read clockwise to find a two-word phrase.

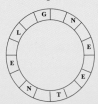

6. Complete the palindrome below .

A_ _ _ _ _ D_ _ _ _ _ _ _ L _ _ S_E_ _A

Clue: *Name change*

7. Fill in the missing numbers to the square at right.

1	1	2	1	0	2	1
2	0	1	2	1	1	0
1	0	1	1	2	1	0
1	2	1	1	0	1	2
0	2	1			1	2
1	1	0			0	1
2	1	0	2	1	0	1
0	1	2	0	1	2	1

8. Unscramble the three anagrammed words below to find three words of the same theme.

STAIR, BULGE, GROAN

10. What comes next in the sequence below?

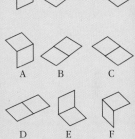

A   B   C

D   E   F

11. Which is the odd one out?

ORB, CIRCLE, RING, CYLINDER, SPHERE

9. Insert the numbers 1–5 in the circles, using each number once, in such a way that for any particular circle, the numbers in the circles connected directly to it add up to the value allocated to the number inside the circle in accordance with the example below.

1 = 4
2 = 12
3 = 2
4 = 8
5 = 6

EXAMPLE:
1 = 14 (4 + 7 + 3)
4 = 8 (7 + 1)
7 = 5 (4 + 1)
3 = 1

12. Find the starting point and move vertically or horizontally, but not diagonally, from letter to letter to spell out a seventeen-letter phrase.

L	L	B		
E	O	O		
B	K	A	C	A
	N	D	N	
	E	L	D	

13. What letter should replace the question mark?

14. What number should replace the question mark?

5		15
	18	
6		9

4		14
	8	
4		7

3		9
	?	
7		12

15. A phrase has had all its vowels removed and the remaining letters are divided into groups of four. What is the phrase?

CNSR VTNF NRG

16. What comes next in the sequence below?

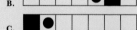

?

A.

B.

C.

D.

17. Make one word using all ten letters below.

MITRE CAROB

Clue: *Atmospheric pressure*

18. 4963 : 79
2835 : 45
What pair of numbers below has the same relationship as the examples above?

A. 4129 : 35
B. 8162 : 94
C. 7411 : 13
D. 2156 : 38
E. 4819 : 52

19. GORY MOMENT is an anagram of which American city?

20. Make up four pairs of words and find the odd one.

MOTOR   CHAIN   WRENCH
MONKEY   CHARM   DAISY
SCHOOL   CRAZY   POOL

21. Take one word from each column to find four compound words. For example: The five words DOOR, STEP, SON, NET, WORK would produce the words DOORSTEP, STEPSON, SONNET, NETWORK.

A	B	C	D	E
MAKE	KEY	LESS	SMITH	DOWN
PIN	SOME	OR	ON	SET
TURN	CROSS	TIME	PLAY	TOP
DOVE	TAIL	WORD	BIT	COST
WAG	SHIFT	BODY	TABLE	LAND

22. Complete the five words so that two letters are common to each word. That is, the same two letters that end the first word also start the second word, and so on. The two letters that end the fifth word are the first two letters of the first word, thus completing the pattern.

_ _ A S _ _
_ _ I B _ _
_ _ G A _ _
_ _ G N _ _
_ _ C H _ _

23. What missing letters should replace the question mark in the square?

OO	TO	TO	FO
OT	TT	TT	FT
OT	TT	TT	FT
OF	TF	TF	?

24. What number should go in D to fit the rule of numbers?

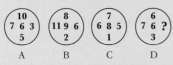

A   B   C   D

25. Trace out a ten-letter word in any direction, using each letter only once.

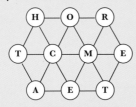

26. Find four words relating to coins by filling in the blanks.

T		M		N
C				B
L		V		E

27. Fill in the missing letters to make a nine-letter word, starting from a corner square and continuing counter-clockwise in a spiral to the center.

A	U	
	Y	O
I	T	L

28. Rearrange the letters in each circle to form two seven-letter words that are synonyms.

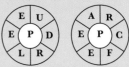

Each word commences with the center letter.

29. Work out the pattern of the route and find out what should replace the question mark.

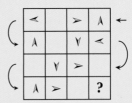

30. Place two of the four-letter groups together to make a word.

YWAY - ROED -
ANAB - ALLE -
ALIC - TYPE

31. Which word means the same as SOPHISTRY?

    (a) TRICK   (c) RIGHTEOUSNESS

    (b) SELFISHNESS   (e) CARELESSNESS

    (c) RIGHTEOUSNESS

32. What is the meaning of QUETZAL?

    (a) BIRD   (c) TOOL   (e) TREE

    (b) MUSICAL INSTRUMENT   (d) DISH

33. Which is the odd one out?

          A   B   C   D

34. If HARDWOOD is to ELM, then SOFTWOOD is to:

    (a) CHERRY   (c) MAHOGANY   (e) BEECH

    (b) PINE   (d) APPLE

35. PEWTER is an alloy made up of which two metals?

    (a) TIN + LEAD   (d) LEAD + NICKEL

    (b) TIN + ZINC   (e) TIN + ALUMINIUM

    (c) LEAD + ZINC

36. Fill in the missing letters to name a group of MUSICIANS.

_ U _ R _ E _

37. Below are the letters that you do not need. Using the missing letters of the alphabet, change their order, and you will find a bird.

ACDFGJKNOPQSTUVXYZ

38. What number should replace the question mark?

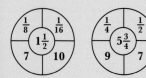

39. Which of these anagrams is not a building?

(a) STILCORE
(b) SILOCMEU
(c) ROGNOD
(d) QUMRAIAU
(e) SABICAIL
(f) TUDANOR

40. Can you find the next position of the bottle that will continue the sequence?

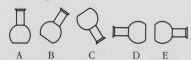

A   B   C   D   E

1. INCOMPREHENSIBLE
2. 30. $7 \times 4 + 2 = 30$
3. PUITN = INPUT
4. D. The figure on the left arm goes inside the figure on the right arm. The remainder of the original goes inside the central figure.
5. WIT. WITLESS, WITNESS
6. All the figures are in anagram pairs except 294, which is therefore the odd one out: 563–635, 916–196, 298–829, 594–945, 752–572, 671–176, 832–283.
7. Laughing all the way to the bank.
8. ALLOT
9. LAUNCH SITE
10. 592. The numbers 48375926 are being repeated in the same order.
11. C. Each connected line of four circles contains one each of the four different symbols.
12. Take the bull by the horns.
13. 35. The numbers represent the position of each letter T in the sentence.
14. 3. The numbers indicated by the hands increase by 7 each time—i.e., 12, 19, 26, 33.
15. NOTABLE, NOT ABLE, NO TABLE
16. (d) WET. Each letter moves forward four places in the alphabet.

S	TUV	W
A	BCD	E
P	QRS	T

17. Tower of strength
18. 6. Each line of the four circles totals 17.
19. D. A facial feature appears in the center when it appears three times in the surrounding circles.
20. SAPPHIRE. These are all "blue" words.
21. D
22. (c) DESPAIR
23. Tutorial
24. C
25. MACKEREL
26. $5/11 \div 25/22 = 5/11 \times 22/25 = 2/5$.
27. Overshadow
28. $29/40$. Divide the top and bottom by 25.
29. (b) MUSOPHOBIA
30. (c) DINNER
31. PITCH
32. 36. We use a mathematical base of 10. If we use 8, we get $64 - 8 - 1$.
    $2 - 0$ (4×4 mod $10 = 16$), but 4×4 mod $8 = 20$.
    Therefore, $3 - 6$ (5×6 mod $10 = 30$), but 5×6 mod $8 \div 36$.
33. C. A = CRYPTS,
    B = LYRICS,
    D = SCRIPT.
34. 6. In each vertical column the three smaller numbers equal the larger number.
35. (d) EXPERT

36. 44. $(8 \times 7) = 56$
$- (2 \times 6) = \underline{12}$
$= 44$

37. (b) TIERCEL (bird)

38. GUPPY, POPPY

39. (c) ≡

40. LOCKJAW

ANSWERS TEST 2

1. SEPTEMBER
ANTI**SEP**TIC
CEN**TI**PEDE
MUL**TIP**LE
JULY

2. 22. Each number is derived by adding the two numbers at either side of it.

3. DEFT THEFT

4. MEAT, STEW, TART, SAGO, BEAN, FLAN, RICE.

5. WEDNESDAY

6. 3. All the other figures have an arrow pointing to their shortest side.

7.

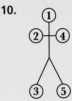

Seven pieces

8. "Many hands make light work."

9. 12

10.

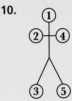

27. Add digits of Circle 2 to obtain Circle 1. Add digits of Circle 1 to obtain Circle 4. Multiply digits of Circle 2 to obtain Circle 3. Multiply digits of Circle 3 to obtain Circle 5.

11. 1. All widgets have a hole in the middle.

12. 12. $9 \times 8 = 72 \div 6 = 12$. Therefore, $9 \times 4 = 36 \div 3 = 12$.

13. All are buildings: LODGE (OGLED), TOWER (WROTE), CASTLE (CLEATS), TEMPLE (PELMET).

14. D. In all the others, the rectangle and black dot are at either side of the arrow. In D, it is the white dot and rectangle.

15. $6\frac{1}{4}$. $(5 \times \frac{1}{2}) \times (10 \times \frac{1}{4})$

16. COMANCHERO

17. (c) THROBBING

18. MA IS AS SELFLESS AS I AM.

19. (c) RISK

20. 315. Multiply by 0.75, 0.5, 0.25, and repeat.

21. 2. The numbers represent the number of rectangles in which they are inside.

22. GERMANE, COGNATE

23. LYCHEE

24. A. Now each line points to a different side or corner.

25. JACK

26. $33. Vowels = $4; consonants = $5.

27. 8. The corresponding segments of each circle add up to 19.
Example: $6 + 11 + 2 = 19$
$7 + 5 + 7 = 19$

28. REFEREES. The missing letters are R and F.

29. (c) 19.635 sq. in.

30. (e) TENDON

31. 63. $(9 \times 9) - (6 \times 3)$

32. $\frac{1}{12}$;

$$\frac{16 \times 9 \times 7 \times 2}{8 \times 18 \times 14 \quad 12} = \frac{2,016}{24,192} = \frac{1}{2}$$

33. It is a wise father that knows his own child.

34. CORSAIR, FELDSPAR

35. C

36. D. The X is midway between a black and white ball.

37. N and M to spell ENUMERATE

38. 36. The differences are:
$2^2 \; 3^2 \; 4^2 \; 5^2 \; 6^2 \; 7^2$

39. ANCESTRY

40. V and F to spell OVERFLOWS

ANSWERS TEST 3

1. THANKSGIVING

2. They all contain the letters ONE in a certain position:

_ ON _ E _	_ _ ON _ E	_ O _ NE _
LONGER	BLONDE	CORNER
MONKEY	BRONZE	LOANED
WONDER	SPONGE	HORNET

3. Four ways.

4. B. This completes every possible arrangement of four blocks, not counting rotations and reflections.

5. C. SOFT

6. 2. In each pentagon,
A + D =
E + B + C

7. Joe

8. SACRAMENTO (ESCORT A MAN)

9. OCCUPANT, RESIDENT

10.

11. 4,146. In all the others, A × C = B and
B + C = D. For example: 36 2 8
ABCD

12.

13. B. The figure is flipped over vertically.

14. ABALONE, ABANDON, ABDICATE,
ABDOMEN, ABOUND, ABROGATES,
ABSCOND

15. RUSH

16. AC(CORD)IAN

17. ENERGETIC, LETHARGIC

18. 12. Add up the three numbers and
reverse—i.e., 7 + 8 + 6 = 21.

19. SLACK, TIGHT

20. D. The final figure at the end of each
row and column is determined by the
contents of the previous two squares.
When a symbol appears in the same
place in both squares it is carried forward but changes from cross to dot,
and vice versa.

21. FIFE, TUBA, LUTE, OBOE.
ODD PAIR: HA

22. 32. Simplify: 5 + (8 ÷ 4) + (9 × 2)
+ 7 = 5 + 2 + 18 + 7 = 32
Order of operations: × ÷ + −

23. PINION

24. JERKIN

25. JOSH, TEASE

26. C. This contains the only ice-cream-cone-
shaped figure that has two black circles
in it.

27. A

28. BERBERIS, CAPSICUM, FOXGLOVE

29. CONE (NICK) KRIS
1 2   2413 3 4
LISP (SOLE) ETON
1 2   2413 3 4

30. (c) 400 ft. (5^2 × 16 = 400)

31. 44. Start at 24, then add 6, then deduct 4,
spiralling in towards the center.

32. (b) 720.   Take pi as $\frac{22}{7}$; then, $\frac{22}{7}$
× 28 = 88 inches
= $\frac{1760 \times 3 \times 12}{88}$ = 720

33. ⊢ They are numbers 1 to 8 with the top
and bottom horizontal lines missing.

34. (b) ∞

35. CHRISTMAS, MAURITIUS, FALKLAND

36. TEN

37. C

38. CABBAGE

39. DECK. QUARTERDECK, DECKHAND

40. D

ANSWERS TEST 4

1. F. All those with one black eye have their curl to the right. All those with a black nose have their curl to the left. All those with neither black eye nor nose have their curl pointing straight up.

2. Intelligently

3. AGE-GROUP, STOCK-STILL, BLOOD-TYPING, TWIN-SIZE

4. Minus $100

5. LEAST

6. 1. The top line plus the bottom line equal the middle line, i.e., 5384968 + 3276873 = 8661841.

7. B. AGATHA, to complete the sequence:

```
_ A _ _ B _
_ C _ _ D _
_ E _ _ F _
_ G _ _ H _
```

8. LET THE CAT OUT OF THE BAG

9. C

10. 10 provinces in Canada

11. ARMADA
WARMTH
CHARMS   XYZ = ARM
DISARM

12. 8. The sum of each column of numbers increases by 1 each time.

13.

14. G and T to spell ORIGINATOR

15. A. It has only one loose end; the others all have two.

16. 1. CAPACITY
2. BRAIN
3. EXPLORING
4. LEARNED

17. PENELOPE

18. 812. $6 + 2 = 8$; $9 + 3 = 12$

19. RETORTS (ORBIT) LIBERTY
2 51   12345 43

20. A bolt from the blue

21. 20. 6, 5, 2, 3, 4. Opposite sides always add up to 7.

22. E. A is the same as C; B is the same as D.

23. (b) SAMOYED (dog). The others are:
(a) QUETZALE, (b) CRUSADO,
(c) BOLIVAR, (d) TESTER,
(e) SESTERCE.

24. COASTER

25. HERMIT, NAUSEA

26. JITTERBUG, QUADRILLE, POLONAISE

27. LADYLIKE, HOYDENISH

28. SLUGGISH, INACTIVE. The missing letters are: S, G, C, and V.

29. (e) BOAT

30. X. Add $2 + 4 + 4 = 10 = X$

31. $11\frac{1}{2}$. There are two series
$(+1\frac{1}{2})$ 7 $8\frac{1}{2}$ 10 $11\frac{1}{2}$
$(-2\frac{3}{4})$ 17 $14\frac{1}{4}$ $11\frac{1}{2}$

32. (e) SCARF

33. (a) ICOSAHEDRON

34. (d) 120°. $\dfrac{360°}{6} = 60°$ = Central Angle.

$180° - 60° = 120°$.

35. -2. $\dfrac{(4 \times 2) - 6}{7 - (4 \times 2)} = \dfrac{2}{-1} = -2$

36. (e) CATS

37. RED

38. SOUBRETTE

39. C. A = PRIZES;
  B = CREPES or CREEPS;
  D = PRECIS or PRICES

40. (e) FOOD

ANSWERS TEST 5

1. MAT
  ✳ between words means anagram
  ➤ between words means add a letter
  ★ between words means change first letter

2. They all contain names of animals:
  A(MULE)T,
  D(EMU)RE,
  MO(RAT)ORIUM,
  MUL(TIGER)M

3. A. This completes every possible permutation of the original square where none of the four symbols occupy the position they held in the original square.

4. B. ESCAPADE

5. ICEBREAKER

6. He loved Vienna. He hated places whose names are made up of two three-letter words: MAD-RID, WAR-SAW, ANT-RIM.

7. 21. All the others are in 1:3 ratio pairs:15–45, 9–27, 18–54, 8–24.

8.

8	6	2
4	T	7
5	1	3

9. VICUNA. All the others are man-made.

10. SLIDE RULE/SLY DROOL

11. RECLAIM, MIRACLE

12. 7.

13. B. The medium-size rectangle is moving from left to right at each stage.

14. WATER, MOVEMENT

15. G. Start at the left-side letter R and jump clockwise to alternate segments to spell out the word "regular."

16. C. It is a mirror image of the opposite square.

17. Nine. Thirty-one people pay $2.27 each. $9 \times 31 = \$70.37$.

18. PEACE

19. 3,205

20.

D O	P B I	O N
E M	F	S T
H E B	M Y I A	M O A O
S E A	O T A M	S R O T

↑

Start at the letter indicated and spiral clockwise around the perimeter to spell out "mashed potato."

21. A

22. KHAKI, IGUANA

23. (a) .875. They read as follows: $\frac{1}{2}, \frac{2}{3}, \frac{3}{4}, \frac{4}{5}, \frac{5}{6}, \frac{6}{7}$.

24. (e) BALE

25. DUNLIN

26. $\frac{6}{7}$. $\frac{1}{3} \div \frac{7}{18} = \frac{1}{3} \times \frac{18}{7} = \frac{6}{7}$.

27. C. The other examples comprise pairs of numbers and one of their factors.
A $13 \times 4 = 52$
$37 \times 10 = 370$
$23 \times 5 = 115$

B $22 \times 4 = 88$
$16 \times 7 = 112$
$17 \times 8 = 136$
C $15 \times 6 = 90$
$24 \times 6 = 144$
$19 \times 10 = 190$, *not* 290

28. 1. S; it is the only letter not made of straight lines.
2. N; it is the only letter made up of straight lines.
3. D; it is the only letter not made of straight lines.

29. (c) CALABASH (fruit)

30. MISSEL THRUSH

31. The circles are in sets of three in different orders:

32. SLOWWORM

33. (a) HODOPHOBIA

34. CUR, RAT, APE

35. (c) 108°. $\frac{360°}{5} = 72° =$ Central Angle. $180° - 72° = 108°$.

36. $3\frac{1}{2}$. $(5 \times \frac{1}{10}) + (12 \times \frac{1}{4})$

37. INGRAINED

38. $1365 = \frac{15 \times 14 \times 13 \times 12 \times 11 \times 10 \times 9 \times 8 \times 7 \times 6 \times 5}{1 \times 2 \times 3 \times 4 \times 5 \times 6 \times 7 \times 8 \times 9 \times 10 \times 11}$

39. L is the same number of letters away from
E & S
B & V
G & Q

40. 0.375

1.

C	M	A	G	I
A	G	I	C	M
I	C	M	A	G
M	A	G	I	C
G	I	C	M	A

2. Hit the nail on the head.

3. 30 mph.
210 miles ÷ 30 = 7 hours
210 miles ÷ 35 = 6 hours

4. D. The rest are all the same figure rotated.

5. 8. Looking along each row and down each column the sums of alternate numbers are the same. For example: 9 + 6 = 4 + 11; 9 + 5 = 3 + 11.

6. STUDY

7. GAUNT

8. IDENTICALLY ELECTING POET

9. SEPTEMBER. Start at JANUARY and jump one month, then two months, then three months, etc.

10. R. Take the left-hand letter from the top row and the right-hand letter from the bottom row added to ATE to spell EATEN. Then work left to right on the top and right to left on the bottom to spell out the words: EATEN, WATER, LATEX, HATED, DATED, GATES, and CATER.

11. D. Working counterclockwise around the larger circles, the shaded quadrant moves one place clockwise. Working clockwise round the smaller circles, the shaded quadrant moves one place counterclockwise.

12. 150.
38 × 2 (+2) = 78
39 × 2 (+2) = 80
58 × 2 (+2) = 118
74 × 2 (+2) = 150

13. FACULTY

14. 24. The numbers, spelled out, follow the numerical sequence: 3-4-5-6-7-8-9-10. One, four, seven, eleven, fifteen, thirteen, seventeen. So the answer is 24—i.e., twenty-four = 10 letters.

15. GEORGINA. REIN AGOG is an anagram of Georgina; REAR LION is an anagram of Lorraine.

16. B. In all the others the outer figure is the same as the inner figure.

17. A. The red ball

18. ODD ONE OUT

19. STRATAGEM

20. MENDELSSOHN

21. 77. After the third number, each number is the total of the three preceding numbers.

22. 5. 6 × 9 = 54   54 − 5 = 49
Similarly, (7 × 4) − 4 = 24
(3 × 9) − 8 = 19

23. APSE.
ROPE (PART) ANTE
3 1   1234 2   4
SHAM (APSE) PIER
3 1   1234 2 4

24. 15. We use a mathematical base of 10. If we use 7, we get $49 - 7 - 1$. Therefore, $2 - 4$ (3×6 mod $10 = 18$), but 3×6 mod $7 = 24$.
$1 - 5$ (4×3 mod $10 = 12$), but 4×3 mod $7 = 15$.

25. 5.
$$\frac{24}{1 + 4 + 3} = 3$$
$$\frac{18}{1 + 4 + 1} = 3$$
$$\frac{30}{1 + 4 + 5} = 3$$

26. HILDEGARDE

27. POACH

28. (c) 10

29. MONEYMAKER

30. ODIOUS, MURDER

31. (d) $\frown$

32. $7\frac{1}{2}$. There are two series:
$(+ 2\frac{1}{4})$ 1 $3\frac{1}{4}$ $5\frac{1}{2}$ $7\frac{3}{4}$
$(-1\frac{1}{2})$ 12 $10\frac{1}{2}$ 9 $7\frac{1}{2}$

33. ROUGHCAST

34. $\frac{27}{40}$. Divide the top and bottom by 25.

35. ADELE, ANNIE, ELIZA, ERICA

36. FUZZY-WUZZY

37. SIGNALMAN, GONDOLIER, MANNEQUIN

38. The numbers increase by 1, 2, 3, etc. The difference between the letters is 2, 3, 5 and 8, respectively, according to the number in the diamond.

$\begin{array}{c} G \\ \hline 8 \end{array}$

39. PIN

40. (b) 15

ANSWERS TEST 7

1.

2. RECONDITE, DARK

3. SUPPORTER, ADVERSARY

4. B. A = DOE (EVIL-DOERS)
C = BEAR (BE ARMED)
D = EWE (BEJEWELLED)
E = APE (TRAP EASILY)

5. 3̣10. Looking around the circles:
2̣5 and 3̣2 = 84
    by adding 5 + 3 = 8
             2 + 2 = 4
3̣2 and 7̣3 = 96
    by adding 2 + 7 = 9
             3 + 3 = 6
7̣3 and 5̣1 = 88
by adding 3 + 5 = 8
             7 + 1 = 8
Therefore: 5̣1 + 2̣5 = 310
    by adding 1 + 2 = 3
             5 + 5 = 10

6. B.

7. CLEAVER. It is a cutting tool whereas the rest are drilling tools.

8. C.

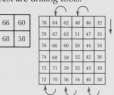

Move from 32 to 78 by the route shown in the sequence: + 3, − 1, + 2.

9. MUESLI

10. All have two meanings when spelled the same but pronounced differently:
APPROPRIATE (take possession of, suitable)
BOW (and arrow, to the King)
DESERT (leave alone, Sahara)
DOVE (dived, bird)
ENTRANCE (door, delight)

GILL (unit of volume, organ of fish)
LEAD (pipe, astray)
SLAVER (slave trader, drool)

11. 9.

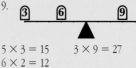

5 × 3 = 15   3 × 9 = 27
6 × 2 = 12
       27

12. B. The top half is folded over onto the bottom half.

13. C. The shaded figures represent 0.75 and 0.5.
72 × 0.5 = 36
68 × 0.75 = 51

14. HERE, THERE

15. C is missing to spell the word "circle."

16. CROSS-EXAMINATION

17. CHARLESTON

18. 37.5 minutes.
$$\frac{50 \times 6}{8} = \frac{300}{8} = 37.5$$

19. D. The third counter from the top disappears at each stage.

20. OFFICIOUS

21. (B) SILK FABRIC

22. ALUMINUM, MANGANESE, MAGNESIUM

23. DEPRESSED

24. A. REEL, so that it spells: 1-2-3. <u>SON</u>, <u>EAT</u>, <u>WORTH</u>, <u>REEL</u>.

25. C

26. D and E. They cannot be folded into a cube.

27. (C) ZINC

28. VOLATILE

29. OBSTETRICS

30. HOTELIER. The missing letters are H and L.

31. 142. The differences are:

1×19	2×19	3×19
19	38	57
4×19	5×19	6×19
76	95	114

32. Here today, gone tomorrow.

33. 4. Subtract the sum of the outside numbers from the sum of the inside ones.
$$(6 + 7 + 7 + 4) - (2 + 1 + 9 + 8)$$

34. RED

35. PADDLING

36. (D) IRREVERENCE

37. WINTER CHERRY

38. JALOPY

39. A family that prays together stays together.

40. 9. $\dfrac{3 \times 7 \times 3}{7}$

ANSWERS TEST 8

1. A. The dot moves down at each stage, first jumping one square, then two, then three. A square turns black once it has been visited by the dot.

2. 11. The right-hand circle contains the sum of pairs of digits from the three-figure number in the left-hand circle and vice versa—i.e., 378. 3 + 7 = 10; 3 + 8 = 11; 7 + 8 = 15.

3. SPEND, HOARD

4. GRIDIRON, WORKLOAD, FIREWOOD, MAINLAND

5. 468137. The even numbers and then odd numbers from the first number are placed in ascending order to form the second number.

6. They all contain the names of countries: L<u>IBERATION</u>: IRAN; <u>INITIALLY</u>: ITALY; F<u>RANCE</u>: FRANCE; <u>CHINCHILLA</u>: CHINA; S<u>PEARMINT</u>: SPAIN; <u>PERFUME</u>: PERU; C<u>LAUSTROPHOBIA</u>: AUSTRIA

7. W. It has twenty-two letters in the alphabet before it, and three letters after it.

8. GATEMAN'S NAME TAG

9. SPRING

10. Bend over backwards

11. 2. Looking both across and down, the sum of each pair of numbers is one more than that of the previous pair of numbers.

12. XYZ = RAP.
RAPIDS,
DRAPES,
SCRAPE,
ENTRAP

13. LONE, LOAN

14. F, J, J, N. They are the initial letters of the months of the year.

15. MINUET. All the words are dances.

16. D. All the others are made up of three identical figures; D is made up of four

17. VANISH

18. GENEROUS,
CHARITABLE,
BENEVOLENT,
KIND

19. IMPRISONMENT. The missing letters are P, N, and T.

20. LLAMA, SKATE

21. MINE: MINERAL, EMINENT

22. SPITEFUL

23. (b) EXCITING. Each word commences with the last letter of the previous word.

24. PAJAMA

25. 0.875

26. (D) ULNA

27. HOSPITABLE

28. (C) ENTRAILS

29. AGE

30. (C) Cr

31. CLUTTER

32. HAMBURGER,
MINCEMEAT,
SPAGHETTI

33. (D) MOUNTAINS

34. TOKEN.

BATH	SALTS
GREEN	PEPPERS
ICE	FLOE
MAGIC	SQUARE

35. (E) DUMPLINGS

36. (D) DEACON

37. (B) PICTURE POSTCARDS

38. 2 hours. $6 \text{ hrs} = \frac{1}{6} = .167$

$3 \text{ hrs} = \frac{1}{3} = .333$

$.167 + .333 = 0.5$

$\frac{1}{0.5} = 2$

39. (C) CLUB SHAPED

40. 52. $(12 \times 5) = 60 - (4 \times 2) = 52$

1.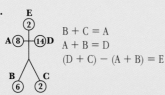

2. CHAPERON

3. 15. +0, +1, +2, +3, then repeated.

4. CUPID WAS THE GREEK GOD OF LOVE. False; he was a Roman god.

5. 15 minutes

6. FASHION

7. LEXINGTON. The three-letter words formed are: NIL, ACE, MIX, OBI, TAN, SAG, CAT, WOO, BAN.

8. 90° in a right angle

9. SEVEN

10. MORBID HEAP

11. DRINKING FOUNTAIN

12.

E ② A ⑧ ⑭ D B ⑥ C ②

$B + C = A$
$A + B = D$
$(D + C) - (A + B) = E$

13. CRITICISM

14. They are all portmanteau words—i.e., words formed by combining parts of other words: GLIMMER (GLEAM, SHIMMER), CHORTLE (CHUCKLE, SNORT), MOTEL (MOTOR, HOTEL), FLOUNDER (FLOUNCE, FLOUNDER)

15. D. Add a point to an existing line, then add another line with the first arrowhead pointing to the left.

16. CLAVICLE

17. 7.

	4		9
⑦	12	8	

18. GALA – PAGEANT (NEAT + GAP)

19. Chain of command

20. (E) 10^9

21. Success is getting what you want. Happiness is liking what you get. —H. Jackson Brown

22. TOR. OPERATOR, TORUS

23. BURIED TREASURE

24. (A) ANTELOPE

25. GINKGO

26. OKRA, KALE, LEEK, BEET. ME is not used

27. (C) CHANSON (song). The others are: (A) CHIHUAHUA, (B) PAPILLON, (D) ELKHOUND, (E) SALUKI, (F) CORGI.

28. HEN, EMU, LOON

29. SEPARATE, DISUNITE. The missing letters are S, P, D, and N.

30. (D) NARROW NECK

31. Thirty-two

32. -35.
$8 - (6 \times 7) - (10 \div 5) + 1$
$8 - 42 - 2 + 1 = -35$
Order that calculation must be made in: $\times \div + -$

33. HEEDFUL, OBLIVIOUS

34. C. A = LAPSES; B = PLACES; D = PLEASE.

35. KAMPONG

36. 8. The numbers are in sets of 3 that add up to 20 each time.

37. TOP

38. RHESUS MONKEY

39. 153. The differences are:
$-11 \quad -22 \quad -33$
$-44 \quad -55 \quad -66$

40. (C) ANNOYANCE

ANSWERS TEST 10

1. 1. Start with the 4 on the outer rim at the top. The total of each straight line of 4 numbers working clockwise is 9, 10, 11, 12, 13, 14, 15, 16.

2. VIGOR

3. OVER

4. D. Now each three adjacent blocks spell out a three-letter word:
ADO, FOE,
DOE, DUE,
ELF, FEE,
SEE, USE,
SUN.

5. DETECTIVE STORIES

6. -1. $\dfrac{-7 \times 3 \times 2}{3 \times 2 \times 7} = \dfrac{-42}{42} = -1$

7. B. Starting at the top and working downwards, the third hexagon in each side of three hexagons is made up of everything in the previous two hexagons, except where the same component appears twice, in which case it is not carried forward.

8. CONCAVE,
BULGING

9. He laughs best who laughs last.

10. FIRST. Each word contains three consecutive letters of the alphabet.

11. 6. $7 \times 3 \times 3 = 63$,
$7 \times 5 \times 1 = 35$,
$4 \times 2 \times 2 = 16$.

12. 13. The values are:

$\diamondsuit$ 3

$\heartsuit$ 8

$\spadesuit$ 2

$\clubsuit$ 1

13. SUSQUEHANNA

14. On top of the world

15. GERTRUDE STEIN

16. BEECH,
CEDAR,
PLANE,
MAPLE,
LARCH

17. $\frac{2}{7}$. $\frac{1}{4} \div \frac{7}{8} = \frac{1}{4} \times \frac{8}{7} = \frac{2}{7}$.

18. 138, 135, 141, 138.
In each pair of rows:
A + C = F   B + D = G
A + D = E   B + C = H

A	B	C	D
E	F	G	H

19. 5935. In the others, the first two digits multiplied give you the last two digits. For example: $5 \times 7 = 35$ (5735).

20. WRY: DOWRY, WRYNECK

21. ELAND, REINDEER, ZEBU, ANTELOPE, BUFFALO. Sixth animal: ZEBRA.

22. (E) ZIGZAG

23. 6%

24. MICROSCOPE

25. (a) PLUMP

26. MIDSHIPS

27. DESTROYER,
MINELAYER,
TROOPSHIP

28. APHELION

29. 43. It is a series of prime numbers.

30. Seven at 50¢, three at $1.50, and two at $2

31. (e) 135°. $\frac{360°}{8} = 45°$ = Central Angle.
$180° - 45° = 135°$.

32. C. A is the same as D; B is the same as E.

33. (e) +

34. (c) SITOPHOBIA

35. 16 lbs. ($128 \div 8 = 16$)

36. SPRUCE

37. (c) 20°C. $68°F - 32° = 36° \times \frac{5}{9} = 20°$

38. (e) SLANG

39. PRONOUNCED

40. 120. $5 \times 4 \times 3 \times 2 \times 1$

1. T(HAIL)AND

2.

G R	A	D	E
R I	L	E	D
A L	I	B	I
D E	B	I	T
E D	I	T	S

3. Once. The vowel is E.

4. 3. $347 \times 2 = 694$; $489 \times 2 = 978$; $267 \times 2 = 534$.

5. RADIUS. It is in the arm; the rest are in the leg.

6. 7. All the numbers are the number of straight lines in each word.

7. FIRE
AFFIDAVIT
GRAVITATE
AGITATOR
LONGITUDE
SITUATION
WATER

8. 300. They are times in hours and minutes without the colon. Starting at 150 (1:50), move clockwise adding 35 minutes at each stage: 1:50, 2:25, 3:00, 3:35, 4:10, 4:45, 5:20, 5:55.

9. B. At each stage the third and fifth figures move to the end.

10. PALINDROMICAL (I'M ON RAPID CALL). NURSE I SPY GYPSIES RUN is a palindrome.

11. Might-have-beens

12. D. The vertical curved arms move from left to right and right to left, respectively, by an equal amount each time.

13. RATTLES

14. LARGE

15. 8. $6 - (3 \times 2) + (8 \div 4) + 6 = 6 - 6 + 2 + 6 = 8$.
Order that calculation must be made in: $\times \div + -$

16. 16. Start at 1 and move clockwise, jumping over two spaces and adding 3 each time.

17. C. It has only two small white circles; the rest have three.

18. 2 min., 15 secs. $(1.25 + 0.25) \times {}^{60}/_{40}$

19. LEAN, AND. WITH, THIN. GEM, EMIT. Musical word: ANTHEM.

20. A. It spirals counterclockwise. The others all spiral clockwise.

21. 498. 6×83

22. (d) WHALES

23. $^{7}/_{40}$. Divide the top and bottom by 25.

24. KEYBOARD. Each word commences with the middle two letters of the previous word.

25. (b) TAP

26. MINION

27. (e) MADRIGAL

28. WREATH, SENILE

29. SPOON

30. ATTIC,
ERECT,
CRYPT,
AISLE

31. FRANGIPANI

32. SEASONED

33. (b) Σ

34. GAMIN, URCHIN

35. CONCH, LANCE

36. (a) OPPOSE

37.

```
  /\
 /  \
/  J \
\ 32 /
 \  /
  \/
```

The series are as follows:
A(bc)D(ef)G(hi) J
17(18-19-20)21(22-23-24-25)26(27-28-29-30-31)32

38. CATCHWORD

39. HER

40. GASTROPOD

ANSWERS TEST 12

1. Imagination

2. C. A has the same figures as D upside down; B has the same figures as E upside down.

3. Rub up the wrong way.

4. Add lines into the position as shown in the original figure.

5. ALLAY, ROUSE

6. C. Some widgets have a straight edge.

7. 14. The numbers in boxes are the sums of two of the numbers in circles: 8 + 5 = 13; 8 + 9 = 17; 5 + 9 = 14.

8. OPPRESS, OPPOSITION, OPPORTUNE.

9. MEDDLESOME

10. BELL,
HARP,
LUTE,
FIFE

11. B. Each line across and down contains one each of the four symbols.

12. 24. Go counterclockwise around the circles and finish in the center. The first set adds 2 to each circle, the second set adds 3, the third set 4, and the fourth set 5.

13. PETULANT

14. SENILE FELINES

15. Seventeen

16. DAPPLE-GRAY

17. GRAND,
    GRAPH,
    GREAT,
    GUIDE,
    GUANO

18. SHEET-WRAP,
    LAPEL-TURN,
    NUT-CRACK,
    PAPER-WRITE

19. E. Opposite segments have lines in the opposite direction—i.e., horizontal becomes vertical and vice versa.

20. Purple. The colors start with the numerical position of each letter in the alphabet.

21. MAGNOLIA. HEM, SPA, PEG, PIN, TOO, AIL, SKI, TEA

22. 36. The differences are:
    $1\frac{1}{2}$ 3 $4\frac{1}{2}$ 6 $7\frac{1}{2}$ 9.

23. OVERTAKE. The missing letters are V and K.

24. (d) 102.
64	32	16	8	4	2	1
1	1	0	0	1	1	0

25. (d) ELLIPSE

26. $-$. They are in sets of four:
    $\times\ -\ +\ \div$.

27. BAR

28. 3E

29. 22. We use a mathematical base of 10. If we use 9, we get $81 - 9 - 1$. Therefore, $2 - 6$ (6×4 mod $10 = 24$), but 6×4 mod $9 = 26$.
    $2 - 2$ (5×4 mod $10 = 20$), but $5 - 4$ mod $9 = 22$.

30. $2\frac{1}{4}$. There are two series:
    $(-4\frac{1}{4})$ 15 $10\frac{3}{4}$ $6\frac{1}{2}$ $2\frac{1}{4}$
    $(+2\frac{1}{8})$ 1 $3\frac{1}{8}$ $5\frac{1}{4}$

31. (f) WISP

32. UNDERBID

33. (f) EPHEMERA (insect)

34. DACE,
    TOPE,
    ANGEL

35. RANSACK,
    RUMMAGE

36. (b) 59°F.
    $15°C \times \frac{9}{5} = 27° + 32° = 59°F.$

37. Winning isn't everything, it's the only thing.

38. DISPATCHER

39. SCARAB BEETLE

40. ANTARCTICA

1. FINALE
2. JR. All the other pairs are the same distance from the beginning and end of the alphabet, respectively.
3. ASK. DAMASK, ASKANT
4. TRAFALGAR SQUARE
5. A. The diagonal line moves one forward and two back at each stage. The dot moves two forward, then one back.
6. REVERENT
7. DIVISIBILITY
8. 1. In each pair of lines,
   AG + CI = BH; DJ + FL = EK.
   For example: 29 + 36 = 65;
   28 + 63 = 91.

A	B	C	D	E	F
G	H	I	J	K	L

9. FEAR, SOME, WHERE, EVER, MORE: FEARSOME, SOMEWHERE, WHEREVER, EVERMORE
10. BRIGANTINE
11. A. It contains four squares. The number of squares in each figure increases by one each time.
12. (i) ENCOUNTER
    (ii) SEMINAR
    (iii) FORUM
    (iv) CAUCUS
    (v) SUMMIT
    (vi) CONFERENCE
    (vii) AUDIENCE
    (viii) RALLY
    (ix) SYNOD
13. MEDIATE
14. PIE
    DIE
    DUE
    HUE
    HUMBLE
15. LESS
16. Up to a point
17. ENACT.
    NECTAR (ENACT) CARPET
    2 14   1 2 3 4 5   3   5
18. A
19. MEATY.

CRAZY	GANG
APPLE	TURNOVER
FIRST	POST
CHINA	SEAS

20. TREBLE. All are music symbols.
21. $\frac{37}{40}$. Divide the top and bottom by 25.
22. C. Each row and column contains four black and four white dots.
23. 1 banana = 5¢.
    $3a + 4b = 29$
    $1a + 8b = 43$

    $(3a + 4b = 29)$
    $(3a + 24b = 129$
    $\quad -20b = 100$
    $\qquad b = 5$

24. 22 minutes before 12 noon was 11:38 AM. 70 minutes before it was 10:28 AM.

25. ORNATE, TEDIUM, UMPIRE, RECEDE, DEBTOR

26. PILLAGE, PLUNDER

27. PIQUET

28. D ♤

29. 0.0625

30. OBFUSCATE

31. TRIBULATION, HAPPINESS

32. IMPOSTER, DECEIVER. The missing letters are M, S, D, and V.

33. (a) YELLOW

34. DIHEDRAL

35. BADMINTON, WRESTLING, BILLIARDS

36. 21.
$10 + (12 \div 4) + (2 \times 9) - 10 =$
$10 + 3 + 18 - 10 = 21$
Order that calculation must be made in: $\times \div + -$

37. DULCET, SWEET

38. (e) CYNOPHOBIA

39. SWADDLES, POCHARD, INITIALLY

40. (c) BELIEFS

ANSWERS TEST 14

1. B. The symbol with the cross always moves to the opposite corner and the symbol occupying that corner moves across to the previously unoccupied space, taking the cross with it.

2. Center of gravity

3. Start at the H in the top left-hand corner and jump to alternate letters. After reaching the bottom right, return to the second letter on the top row and continue jumping to alternate letters to spell out the phrase "Here today, gone tomorrow." The missing letter is O.

4. 8. Add each of the numbers in the hexagon, then divide by 3 to get the number in the diamond.

5. DOUSED/DUE. All the others are paired whereby the three-letter words are spelled out by the second, fourth, and sixth letters of the six-letter words: AIL/FACIAL, NOD/UNFOLD, LID/ALLIED, RIM/TRUISM, USE/PURSUE, WAS/SWEARS, FEE/EFFETE, EAT/DEPART.

6. THE ANCIENT INHABITANTS OF THE AREA IN CENTRAL ITALY NOW KNOWN AS TUSCANY WERE CALLED ETRUSCANS. True.

7. B. Opposite segments are identical but with black/white reversal.

8. 30 min. 20 miles at 40 mph = $\frac{20}{40} \times 60 = 30$ min.
30 miles at 60 mph = 30 min.

9. Reinvent the wheel

10. WEASEL

11. ROALD AMUNDSEN

12. 47.
$7 \times 3 = 21 \quad 4 \times 9 = 36$
$63 \div 7 = 9 \quad 35 \div 5 = 7$
$2 \times 2 = 4$
$56 \div 8 = 7$

13. MINE, RUSH, DISC: Can all be prefixed by GOLD.
BOMB, ZONE, SCALE: Can all be prefixed by TIME.
BACK, SAIL, ASIDE: Can all be prefixed by SET.
WISE, WORK, TOWER: Can all be prefixed by CLOCK.

14. She originally had $99.98 and spent $49.99.

15.

2	8	5
4	6	T
7	1	3

16. A

17. $11\frac{3}{4}$. There are two series:
$(3\frac{1}{4}) \quad 2 \quad 5\frac{1}{4} \quad 8\frac{1}{2} \quad 11\frac{3}{4}$
$(-2\frac{1}{4}) \quad 12 \quad 9\frac{3}{4} \quad 7\frac{1}{2}$

18. MASTER, STREAM

19. 2. Primes: $29 + 37 = 66$
Squares: $4 \times 16 = 64$

20. CUSTARD PIE

21. GREEN

22. MUTUAL ADMIRATION SOCIETY

23. B. A is the same as D. C is the same as E.

24. It should be blank. Starting from the bottom right-hand corner, move counter-clockwise in a spiral to follow the sequence:
1 2 3 4
∘ ∘ •   •

25. SWEET

26. COMEDIAN

27. $2\frac{1}{2}$. $(18 \times \frac{1}{6}) - (6 \times \frac{1}{12})$

28. (a) BARS

29. FOIL

30. (d) $\sqrt{}$

31. (c) INSIPID

32. BONGO, CANOE

33. (a) FIR

34. (c) STALLION + A SHE ASS

35. HARRAS

36. D. A = MELEES;
B = LESSEE; C = LEASES.

37. MELODEON

38. MANGEL-WURZEL

39. CAIN, ABEL, ADAM, NOAH. AC is not used.

40. FAR-FETCHED

1. B. This is the only one in which the dot is not in both the triangle and circle.

2. ENTANGLE, SEPARATE

3. INTERACTIVE

4. D. In all the other figures, there are exactly twice as many straight lines as curved lines.

5. D. 3 chances in 4. The possibilities of drawing the balls are black/black, white/white, black/white, and white/black. The only one of the four possible combinations where black does not occur is white/white. The chances of drawing at least one black ball is, therefore, three chances in four.

6. A. All the figures contain one right angle.

7. 31

8. LINOCUT. The vowels A, E, I, O, U are being repeated in the same order.

9. HINTED

10. 124986. The positions of the numbers change in the following sequence:
(1 2 3 4 5 6)
9 4 1 6 8 2
(3 6 2 1 5 4)
1 2 4 9 8 6

11. They are all weather words:
REST(RAIN)ED, D(WIND)LE,
COUNTER(SUN)K, SKILLI(GALE)E.

12. Knowledge

13.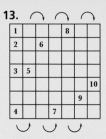

Move as shown counting 1 space, then 2, then 3, etc. between numbers.

14. PANAMA CANAL

15. FIRSTLY

16. B. From top to bottom, the pieces are placed in the order: A, D, H, E, G, C, F, B.

17. AFFIRM, RECANT

18. NEWNESS: NE/W/NE/S/S

19. VOGUE

20. T. The letter that follows each number is the first letter of the number spelled out.

21. WAREHOUSE. All the other words contain THE.

22. 87. $(7 \times 9) = 63 + (4 \times 6) = 24$
$63 + 24 = 87$

23. (e) GRAPHIC. Each word commences with the last letter of the previous word.

24. (e) VERMILLION

25. $\frac{2}{9}$.
$\frac{1}{7} \div \frac{9}{14} = \frac{1}{7} \times \frac{14}{9} = \frac{2}{9}$

26. (d) LEARNED

27. (e) CROWS

28. LEGEND, OUTLAW

29. (f) INTAGLIO (gem). The others are:
(a) NIZAM, (b) SIRDAR, (c) CALIPH,
(d) MULLAH, (e) WAZIR.

30. IGNOMINY, HONOR

31. KENNEL

32. 3. $(12 - 9) \times (3 \div 3) = 3$

33. CABANA

34. (a) MOIDORE (coin)

35. J. Using their numerical positions in the alphabet, the two series go as follows:

+4: B, F, J, N, R
−4: Z, V, R, N, J

36. (e) SOFT

37. INCENSE, INFLAME

38. (d) RICHNESS

39. EUCALYPTUS

40. (d) FUNAMBULIS (tightrope walker)

ANSWERS TEST 16

1. B. The pattern follows the changing position of the sections inside the figure. The lines previously at the left move to the right. The lines in the middle move to the left and the lines at the right move to the middle.

2. ECSTASY, OPPRESSION

3. DEVIL'S ADVOCATE

4. A.
7219 : 126.
$7 \times 2 \times 1 \times 9 = 126.$

5. NEVER ODD OR EVEN

6. Shrinking violet

7. HP. Adding the numerical values of the letters in the alphabet, each pair of letters totals 26, except for HP, which totals 24.

8. 5. The numbers in each suit total 11.

9. INDIGO, AMBER, LAVENDER, CREAM, LEMON. Sixth color: LILAC.

10. LOAN, LONE

11. T. Start at A and move one place, then

two places, through the alphabet, returning to the beginning of the alphabet after passing Z.

12. C. At each alternate stage, a line becomes curved, moving clockwise.

13. THIN, STOUT

14. F.

15. 50 months. Take the Roman numeral value from the middle of each woman's name: TR(IX)IE, DA(VI)NA, HE(L)EN.

16. STRAIGHTFORWARD. The missing letters are S, H, F, and W.

17. C. In all the others, the black circle is at the top.

18. YEARN, LONG

19. (i) FLOTATION.
(ii) LOGO. (iii) MONOPOLY.
(iv) TRANSACTION.
(v) FACTOR.
(vi) INTANGIBLE.
(vii) INCORPORATE.
(viii) FLAGSHIP. (ix) FLYER.
(x) SYNDIC.
Score a point for six or more correct.
Score a bonus point for all ten correct.

20. C. It is a reflection of the others. The others are all the same figure rotated.

21. 0.3125

22. (c) BIRD

23. The lunatics have taken charge of the asylum.

24. E. These are all three-letter words: ZAP, YAW, WHY, GUY, USE.

25. 41. We use a mathematical base of 10. If we use 6, we get $36 - 6 - 1$. Therefore, $1 - 2$ (4×2 mod $10 = 8$), but 4×2 mod $6 = 12$. $4 - 1$ (5×5 mod $10 = 25$), but 5×5 mod $6 = 41$.

26. 3. $\dfrac{4 + 8 + 8 + 4}{(2 \times 4)} = 3$

27. TWO-PIECE

28. SCULPTURED

29. (a) $128\,{}^4\!/_7°$. ${}^{360}\!/_7° = 51{}^3\!/_7° =$ Central Angle. $180° - 51{}^3\!/_7° = 128\,{}^4\!/_7°$.

30. B

31. GROUSE

32. BUDGERIGAR

33. FLY

34. 22. Reading across, the bottom number in each column disappears and the other numbers drop down.

35. JUBILANT. The missing letters are J and L.

36. APPLAUSE

37. ${}^1\!/_4$. $4 \times 12 = 48 - 8 = 40$, ${}^{10}\!/_{40} = {}^1\!/_4$.

38. (b) NELOPHOBIA

39. SQUARE-RIGGED

40. (d) 40°C. $104°F - 32° = 72° \times {}^5\!/_9 = 40°C$

1. CAN. SCANT, ARCANE, CHICANE, SCANNER.

2. 6. $(23 + 31) \div 9 = 6$.

3. E. A is the same as C with black/white reversed. B is the same as D with black/white reversed.

4. ATLANTIS. The others are all imaginary places of perfection.

5. CHIPMUNK. The three-letter words made are: ARC, ASH, LEI, GAP, RAM, YOU, PEN, AND OAK.

6. An optimist thinks this is the best of all worlds. A pessimist fears the same to be true.   *—Doug Larson*

7. RUN

8. INVOLVED

9. A. Opposite segments are mirror images.

10. HIT OR MISS

11. D. The numbers 1, 3, 7, 8, 9, 4, 2, 6 are being repeated following the route shown.

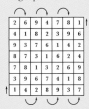

12. VERTEBRAE

13. THAT'S TOUGH, THAT STUFF

14. Pouring oil on troubled waters

15. ARC DE TRIOMPHE

16. VARIATION, DEPARTURE

17. $135. Al's share = $60
= 4 parts
Each part = $15
Original amount = $15 \times 9 = $135

18. CHORUS, USEFUL, ULLAGE, GENIAL, ALLUDE

19. ROCK, CRATER

20. 79. The differences are: $-3\frac{1}{2}$
$-7 \quad -10\frac{1}{2} \quad -14 \quad -17\frac{1}{2} \quad -21$.

21. ROME WAS NOT BUILT IN A DAY

22. WELL-BRED

23. $\frac{11}{12}$. Divide the top and bottom by 75.

24. (b) UNFORTUNATE

25. 55. $5 \times 5 = 1$
$4 \times 4 = 4$
$3 \times 3 = 9$
$2 \times 2 = 16$
$1 \times 1 = 25$

26. BRIDGEHEAD

27. FLUNKYDOM

28. MENAGERIE

29. GNOMON

30. D. A and C are the same; B and E are the same.

31. EDGEWISE

32. CAROB, BURRO

33. (d) 33

34. LAZINESS, IDLENESS.
The missing letters are L, Z, L, and N.

35. BLUES,
SNARE,
STAVE,
BRASS

36. (a) !

37. DISSOLUTE

38. D. A = REPAST or PASTER;
B = PASTOR;
C = RIPEST or STRIPE.

39. D

40. (d) COMPASS

ANSWERS TEST 18

1. C, so that the dot is in two circles.

2. $4\frac{1}{4}$. There are two series:
$(-4\frac{1}{4})$ 17 $12\frac{3}{4}$ $8\frac{1}{2}$ $4\frac{1}{4}$
$(+3\frac{1}{8})$ 8 $11\frac{1}{8}$ $14\frac{1}{4}$

3. CHARACTERIZE. The missing letters are H and Z.

4. BANISH

5. Turn over a new leaf

6. L. The value of the letter is half of the number in the opposite segment. 24 ÷ 2 = 12. L is the twelfth letter of the alphabet.

7. LASZLO BIRO. He invented the ball-point pen.

8. CRUSH, GRIND

9. A. The large figure becomes four small figures that go inside one of the smaller figures previously inside the larger figure.

10. 3

11. SET. All of these words can be prefixed with SUN.

12. WISECRACK (A SICK CREW)

13.

7	4	6	1
8	1	2	7
3	6	1	3
2	9	7	5

14. 258. In the rest the middle digit is the square root of the first and last digits. For example: 4 × 4 = 16 = 146.

15. ELEMENT

16. $4^1/_5$. The opposite sides of a die total 7; the reverse sides are, therefore, 6, 3, 2, 4, 6 = 21.
$21 \div 5 = 4^1/_5$.

17. No, it cannot be determined.

18. BOAT, SHIP, RAFT

19. LEASEHOLD, THRESHOLD, TENEMENTS

20. SIGMUND FREUD

21. 1067. (11×97)

22. POSY.

MONEY	BELT
BUTTER	MILK
PENNY	PINCHING
SALAD	DAYS

23. DALLAS, MOBILE, TOPEKA

24. DOGGER, FISHING, VESSEL

25. C

26. (c) TAMBOUR (drum). The others are: (a) JANIZAR, (b) CHASSEUR, (d) MULETEER, (e) SENTINEL, (f) FUGELMAN.

27. 23. First column: Consecutive odd numbers
Second column: Consecutive square numbers

Third column: Consecutive even numbers
Fourth column: Consecutive prime numbers

28. (d) KNIFE

29. (c) CLOUD

30. BLUEBOTTLE

31. B. It has three symbols in the same position as E.

32. (d) LAND

33. $4^1/_2$ kg.

A: $7^1/_2 \times 4 = 30$
B: $6 \times 2 = 12 + 30 = 42$
C: $12 \times 2 = 24$
D: $4^1/_2 \times 4 = 18 + 24 = 42$

34. TEN

35. FLEECE

36. 10.
$8 + 8 = 16 - (2 \times 3) = 10$

37. $-1^4/_5$.
$$\frac{3 - (4 \times 3)}{(4 \times 3) - 7} = \frac{3 - 12}{12 - 7} = \frac{-9}{5} = -1\frac{4}{5}$$

38. 21. $\dfrac{7 \times 6 \times 2 \times 2}{2 \times 4}$

39. OCTAHEDRAL

40. D. All the rest are divided into four equal segments.

1. 20

2. DESTITUTE

3. RILL. SHRILL, TRILL, DRILL, THRILL, FRILL, GRILL.

4. D. Looking across each line, the black dot moves 45° clockwise at each stage and the circle 45° counterclockwise. Looking down they move the other way around.

5. MILES.
GOSPEL (MILES) IMPOSE
5   3   12345 21   4

6. D. Read around each pair of segments to spell out ORANGE, RAISIN, DAMSON, and CHERRY.

7. TRUMAN, CARTER, PIERCE, MADISON. They were all U.S. presidents.

8. REFEREE. All the others contain an internal rhyme: WAY-LAY, DIS-MISS, FUR-THUR, BACK-PACK.

9. INDIRECT TAXATION

10. E. 532 : 17. $5 \times 3 + 2 = 17$

11. 36 miles.
6 days $\times$ 15 = 90
7 days $\times$ 16 = 112. 112 − 90 = 22 miles.
7 days $\times$ 18 = 126. 126 − 90 = 36 miles.

12. 22. Each number is determined by the two adjacent numbers immediately below it. Add the *numbers* for Rows 3 and 5. For example: Row 5, first two blocks: 73 + 21 = 94.
Add the *digits* for Rows 2 and 4. In Row 2: 5 + 6 + 5 + 6 = 22.

13. BREAK, CRUSH

14. CASE/SEED, VISA/SAKE, HOME/MEAN. Six-letter word: SESAME.

15.

R	A	T	E	D
A	B	I	D	E
T	I	N	G	E
E	D	G	E	D
D	E	E	D	S

16. 210. $7 \times 6 \times 5$

17. They all contain a tree:
UNCL(OAK)ING, DISHW(ASH)ER, CROSS(FIR)E, DO(PINE)SS.

18. JET

19. KILLJOY. The alphabetical sequence F, G, H, I, J moves one position forward in each word.

20. CANDID CAMERA. The three-letter words created: TIC, INN, COD, ODD, TEA, RIM, EVE, AIR.

21. HUMORIST

22. $10\frac{3}{4}$. There are two series:
$(+1\frac{1}{4})$ 7 $8\frac{1}{4}$ $9\frac{1}{2}$ $10\frac{3}{4}$
$(-1\frac{1}{4})$ 12 $10\frac{3}{4}$ $9\frac{1}{2}$

23. SWEETMEATS (SWEDEN). Each word starts with the letters of a country.
    BULLDOG = BULGARIA
    HOLIDAY = HOLLAND
    FRANCHISE = FRANCE
    ITALICS = ITALY

24. SONNET

25. (c) 77°F. 25°C × $\frac{9}{5}$ = 45° + 32° = 77°F.

26. STAR

27. METEORITE, SUPERNOVA, SATELLITE

28. APPEASE, ASSUAGE

29. ADZE, FORK, FILE, JACK. SP is not used.

30. B

31. 2997. 111 × 27

32. (c) WORDS OF AN OPERA

33. (a) INIQUITOUS

34. SAMPAN

35. POLE

36. E. A is the same as C. B is the same as D.

37. CASTANETS

38. (b) FIBULA

39. 26. Simplify:
    12 + (6 ÷ 2) + (1 × 5) + 6 =
    12 + 3 + 5 + 6 = 26.
    Order that calculation must be made in:
    × ÷ + −

40. 4376. The digits total 20. In the others, they total 18.

ANSWERS TEST 20

1. B. If the box were bisected vertically or horizontally, the top half would be a mirror image of the bottom half, and the right-hand side would be a mirror image of the left-hand side.

2. ODE. WOODEN, CODED, REMODEL, MODERN.

3. (a) 25 : 174 : 1217.
   25 × 7 − 1 = 174;
   174 × 7 − 1 = 1217.

4. LATER.
   ERCTA : REACT
   12345 : 21534
   ALERT : LATER
   12345 : m21534

5. 9 planets in the solar system

6. TABLE
   SABLE
   SALE
   SALT

7. Eight

8. 2. $(19 + 5) \div (37 - 25)$

9. B. The sums of the other clocks' hands add up to a square number.

10. KRONA. These are all units of currency.

11. HER.
ARCHER,
HERRING.

12. KNOWN OCEAN,
NO NOTION

13. B. The square moves 90° clockwise at each stage, and the black portion moves from section to section clockwise.

14. A) FIRST,
B) DOWN,
C) CAST.

15. THE STUDY OF INSECTS IS CALLED ETYMOLOGY. False. Etymology is the study of words.

16. 9. The total number of items purchased is 309 (70 + 83 + 58 + 98). Let's say x is the number of women who purchase 4 items. Then 3(100 − x) is the number of women who purchased 3 items.
$4x + 3(100 - x) = 309$
$4x + 300 - 3x = 309$
$x = 9$.
At least 9 women purchased 4 items.

17. BENDS. BARB, BARE, BARN, BARD, BARS.

18. ZERO

19. WEAK, STURDY

20. B. The circle moves clockwise first by one corner, then by two, then by three, etc.

21. GASTRONOME

22. 322. $(7 \times 7 \times 7) - 21 = 322$.

23. (b) ▲▲▲

24. WRASSE. The initial letters down List A will spell WRASSE.

25. D. It has two symbols in the same position as E.

26. $4/7$. $2/9 \div 7/18 = 2/9 \times 18/7 = 4/7$.

27. (b) MORELLO (fruit)

28. (c) SWAGGER

29. SHELVE, VITRIC

30. (b) ♀

31. 968. 121×8
(11×11)

32. B

33. ANT, BEE, VESPA

34. (d) 144°.
$360°/10 = 36° =$ Central Angle.
$180° - 36° = 144°$.

35. (b) da

36. (e) WAKEFUL

37. LIFELESS, DECEASED. The missing letters are F, L, C, and S.

38. (a) A CAP

39. Either he's dead or my watch has stopped.

40. $1/2$. $(4 \times 1/4) - (2 \times 1/4)$

1. CUT A CAPER

2. C. Jack outscored Jim by more than he outscored Alf. From the information given, we know that Sid scored more than Jack. Jack scored more than Alf, and Alf scored more than Jim. We only know that George scored less than Sid.

A is incorrect because Jack scored more than Alf.

B is incorrect because Jack scored more than Jim.

C is <u>correct</u> because Jack outscored both Alf and Jim, and Alf outscored Jim.

D is not proven because the only thing known about George is that he scored less than the top scorer, Sid.

3. EXULTANT

4. A. MINUTE, B. ARTIST

5. C. MIST, D. TEAR, E. UNIT

6. Some men interpret nine memos

7. Throwing caution to the wind

8. PRIMA DONNA

9. 1. The total of the numbers in each figure equals the number of its sides.

10.

7	4	9	6	3	7
3	6	9	4	7	3
6	3	7	4	9	6
9	4	7	3	6	9
4	9	6	3	7	4
7	3	6	9	4	7

Starting at the bottom right-hand corner

the numbers 74963 are repeated following the route shown.

11. (e) DIVEST. Each word commences with the last letter of the previous word.

12. SKEPTICAL, QUIZZICAL

13. LAMB, PORK, VEAL

14. DIZZY.

POTATO	SALAD
WAR	GAMES
LAUGHING	HYENA
TENNIS	MATCH

15. 13. $7 \times 7 = 49$; $49 - 36 = 13$.

16. OCTAGONAL

17. PERSONAL COMPUTER

18. A. In all the others, the dot is in a downward-pointing triangle.

19. DENNIS, NELL, EDNA, LEON, NEDRA, ANITA, ROLF, FLORA, TINA, ARDEN, NOEL, and ELLEN sinned.

20. Thirty-two

21. C. OCTAHEDRON

22. ANIMALS: CAT, PIG, YAK, ASS

23. OFFICIAL

24. LUPIN, CAPON

25. (b) MUSTER

26. VOLUNTARY

27. 28

28. (a) 30°C. 86°F $- 32° = 54° \times \frac{5}{9} = 30°C$.

29. BRONCHITIS

30. 1944. 216 = 6 × 6 × 6; 9 × 216 = 1944.

31. 0.625

32. SCOW, BRIG, DHOW, HULK. BA is not used.

33. SONOROUS. The missing letters are S and R.

34. DISFROCK

35. SHILLELAGH

36. B. A is the same as C. E is the same as D. F is the same as G.

37. 13. We use a mathematical base of 10. If we use 11, we get 121 − 11 − 1. Therefore, 7 − 4 (9 × 9 mod 10 = 81), but 9 × 9 mod 11 = 74. 1 − 3 (7 × 3 mod 10 = 14), but 7 × 2 mod 11 = 13.

38. FRANKFURTER

39. (b) 400 ft. (5^2 × 16)

40. (c) KIBITKA (vehicle). The others are : (a) MONSOON, (b) SQUALL, (d) TORNADO, (e) ZEPHYR, (f) SIROCCO.

ANSWERS TEST 22

1. INTERCHANGEABILITY

2. SCORED.
TOURIST   (SCORED)
　3　4 1　　123456
SCOLDED
　　2　　6 5

3. 7. The sums in the opposite segments are the same: 7 + 2 = 5 + 4.

4. A. The ellipse reduces in size and goes in the rectangle, which rotates 90°. The circle goes at the bottom of the rectangle.

5. DISCOURAGE, SUPPRESSOR, ENDORSABLE, INHABITANT

6. S. Each letter represents the initial of one of the planets: MERCURY, VENUS, EARTH, MARS, JUPITER, SATURN, URANUS, NEPTUNE, PLUTO.

7. Out of the frying pan into the fire.

8. PART. All the words form another word when read backwards.

9. NO LEMONS, NO MELON

10. It is impossible. In the first half of the journey, you would have used up all the time required to achieve 40 mph average.

11. Thirty

12. BROWSE

13. 9. It has just two checks in the list below:

	Alan	Bill	Conny	David	Eileen	Fiona
1	✓	✓	✓			
2			✓	✓	✓	
3	✓		✓	✓		✓
4		✓	✓		✓	✓
5	✓		✓	✓		✓
6			✓		✓	✓
7	✓			✓	✓	
8				✓		
9	✓	✓				
10					✓	

14. NEW BROOMS SWEEP CLEAN.

15. 45. $45 + 18 = 63$ $63 \div 7 = 9$

16.   MONDAY
CORRES POND
    TRES PASS
    SUR PASS
    THUR SDAY

17. C(HANDEL)IER

18. A. At each stage, each dot moves one arm clockwise.

19. CAYMAN, ASP, TOAD

20. OBSTACLE,
BARRIER,
HURDLE,
HINDRANCE

21. SIDE (SHOW) DOWN (TURN) TAIL (GATE) POST (DATE) LINE

22. (d) HYPNOPHOBIA

23. GRATIFY, GLADDEN

24. 100. The differences are:
2^3 3^3 4^3 5^3 6^3 7^3

25. C. Each section moves to the right one space, two spaces, three spaces, four spaces.

26.

The number in each top triangle is multiplied by 3. The letter in each bottom triangle is increased by one letter more each time.

K (LM)   N (OPQ)   W (STUV)

27. TSETSE

28. A. 972; B. 791. In the other numbers, the first and third digits add up to the second digit.

29. PORRINGER, DISH

30. (b) ILLUMINATION

31. WOODPECKER

32. D

33. (d) TWELVES

34. ALWYN, NIGEL, NEILL, AARON

35. 56. $(7 - 3) \times (9 - 2) \times (1+1)$

36. HIDE

37. 2. $(9 \times \frac{1}{9}) \times (\frac{1}{2} \times 4)$

38. PLUMP, MEAGER

39. D. A = CHICKS; B = CHECKS;
    C = CHUCKS.

40. AUGER, RAZOR, LEVER, ANVIL

ANSWERS TEST 23

1. TY. Read across corresponding sections in each square to spell out four eight-letter words.

A	B
C	D

   A = MACARONI
   B = DECIMATE
   C = APPRAISE
   D = TENACITY

2. TEN. HASTEN, TENACE

3. BROWN — UMBER,
   BLACK — SABLE,
   BLUE — SAPPHIRE,
   GREEN — JADE

4. D. The tip of the triangle is folded over.

5. DISASTER

6. BODY MAGNET

7. AR. BARB, CARD, DARK, EARL, FARM, HARP, MART, RARE, TARN, VARY.

8. 120. 15×8.

9. NARRATIVE, STATEMENT

10. (c) GREY LONER KICK BRICK

11. 20. 5×4.

12. 300 meters

13. D. The five-sided figure moves 90° counterclockwise at each stage. The lightning bolt moves 45° counterclockwise on its pivot on the apex of the figure.

14. BANANA SPLIT

15. AMAZON, ONRUSH, SHEATH, THIRST, STREAM

16. Three

17. OVERPAID

18. BREATHTAKING. The missing letters are: H, K, and G.

19. DOUBLE-DEALER, SPOT-CHECK, DOWN-BOW, CROSS-SECTION

20. GUSTAV MAHLER

21. MILITANT TENDENCY

22. 2.
$$7 - (2 \times 6) + (8 \div 2) + 3$$
$$= 7 - 12 + 4 + 3 = 2$$
   Order that calculation must be made in: $\times \div + -$

23. 8. Each number represents the number of letters in each word of the question.

24. PLOVER

25. CERULEAN

26. $^{14}/_{23}$. Divide the top and bottom by 25.

27. SIDE

28. 5. Add the four nonoverlapping numbers in each circle and divide that number by its overlapping number. The answer for all of them is 9. For example: $^{27}/_{3} = 9$.

29. (b) PARABOLA

30. ANY COLOR AS LONG AS IT'S BLACK.

31. 41. We use a mathematical base of 10. If we use 12, then we get $144 \div 12 - 1$. Therefore, $8 - 3$ (11×9 mod $10 = 99$), but 11×9 mod $12 = 83$. $4 - 1$ (7×7 mod $10 = 49$), but 7×7 mod $12 = 41$.

32. (c) ELEVATOR. All these words alternate vowel/consonant or consonant/vowel.

33. NOSEGAY

34. SYNOD,
DEIST,
TRACT,
SAINT

35. 16. In the adjacent circles:

If the nonoverlapping numbers are odd, add them together.
If the nonoverlapping numbers are even, subtract them.
If the nonoverlapping numbers are odd and even, multiply them.

36. (e) DISAPPROVAL

37. 5. $(8 - 4) \times (10 \div 8)$.

38. (c) PALANQUIN (vehicle)

39. SOUVENIR. The missing letters are S and V.

40. COSTARD. The missing letter is D.

ANSWERS TEST 24

1. D. The portion on the left moves to the right, the portion on the right moves to the top, the portion at the bottom moves to the left, and the portion at the top moves to the bottom.

2. ECU, SEN, PESO

3. MAKE BOTH ENDS MEET

4. 6525. Reverse the last three digits and add it to 6312: $6312 + 213 = 6525$.

5. XYZ = PIT
PITIED,
SPITED,
WAPITI,
PULPIT

6. TESSELLATE

7. ROOK,
HAWK,
COOT,
DOVE

8. MAD – DERANGED (GRADE, END)

9. B

10. A) BACK;
B) HEAD;
C) REST.

11. 17. Start at 2 and, moving clockwise, jump one segment each time adding 1, 2, 3, etc.

12. MADELINE

13. CONFRONTATIONAL. The missing letters are N, R, I, and A.

14. GLOCKENSPIEL

15. BLANDER,
BLENDER,
BLINDER,
BLONDER,
BLUNDER

16. C. The contents of each pentagon are determined by the contents of the two pentagons immediately below it. These contents are merged, but when two lines appear in the same position, they disappear.

17. $2/7$. $4/11 \div 28/22 = 4/11 \times 22/28 = 2/7$.

18. A. SATIRE, B. NORMAL

19. C. NEAR,
D. SORT,
E. MAIL

20. FIRST

21. 4 SUITS IN A DECK OF CARDS

22. C. In all the others, the black dot is third from the left.

23. (e) ZINC

24. (d) WHITEN

25. MIKADO, MALLET

26. (c) 150°. $360°/12 = 30° =$ Central Angle. $180° - 30° = 150°$.

27. 0.6875

28. FLAG, GEUM, ARUM, IRIS. BE is not used

29. 108. $(8 \times 2 \times 7) - 4$.

30. MISTY.

CHAIN	GANG
CHIMNEY	SWEEP
FOX	TROT
TIGER	LILY

31. DUST JACKET

32. B. A is the same as E. C is the same as D.

33. SKIN

34. (b) BANNOCK

35. INHERENT,
ACQUIRED

36. LESS

37. D. It has four dots in the square.

38. SHANTY

39. FORETELL, FORECAST. The missing letters are F, T, F, and C.

40. (c) 122°F. $50°C \times 9/5 = 90° + 32° = 122°F$.

1. TEACH, TEMPO, TEASE, TAMED, TARES

2.

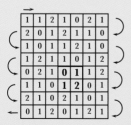

3. GREAT APE, GREY TAPE

4. B. The first four figures are being repeated but only half the figure is shown—first the left-hand half, then the right-hand half.

5. INTELLIGENCE TEST

6. AL LETS DELLA CALL ED STELLA

7. The figures 11210210 are being repeated following the route shown.

8. SITAR, BUGLE, ORGAN

9.

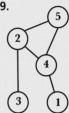

10. B. The horizontal diamond stays in the same position. The other diamond pivots around it clockwise, joining it on a new side each time.

11. CYLINDER

12. BELL, BOOK, AND CANDLE

13. O. The word PASTER, read clockwise around the outer segments, can be altered to form a new word by the letters in the same section in the circle.
PASTER: MASTER, POSTER, PATTER, PASSER, PASTOR, PASTEL

14. 28. (3×12) $(\div 9)$ $(\times 7)$.

15. CONSERVATION OF ENERGY

16. D. The black dot moves two back one forward, the black square moves two forward, one back.

17. BAROMETRIC

18. D. 2156 : 38. Divide the first and second pair of digits by 7 to get the answer: $21 \div 7 = 3$ and $56 \div 7 = 8$ = 38.

19. MONTGOMERY

20. CRAZY.

CHARM	SCHOOL
CAR	POOL
MONKEY	WRENCH
DAISY	CHAIN

21. TURN,
KEY,
WORD,
PLAY,
LAND
TURNKEY,
KEYWORD,
WORDPLAY,
PLAYLAND

22. ERASED,
EDIBLE,
LEGACY,
CYGNET,
ETCHER

23. FF.
OO = One Across, One Down
TO = Two Across, One Down
TT = Two Across, Two Down
or
TT = Three Across, Three Down
FF = Four Across, Four Down, etc.

24. 3. $\frac{6}{3} + 7 - 6 = 3$

25. TACHOMETER

26. TOMAN,
NOBLE,
LIVRE,
TICAL

27. LOQUACITY

28. PRELUDE,
PREFACE

29. A left arrow. Turn 90° clockwise, miss 1 square, turn 180°, and repeat.

30. ALLEYWAY

31. (a) TRICK

32. (a) BIRD

33. C. It has four stars; the others have three stars.

34. (b) PINE

35. (a) TIN + LEAD

36. QUARTET

37. WHIMBREL

38. $1^3/_{16}$.

$(7 \times \frac{1}{8}) + (10 \times \frac{1}{16}) = 1\frac{1}{2}$;

$(9 \times \frac{1}{4}) + (7 \times \frac{1}{2}) = 5\frac{3}{4}$;

$(9 \times \frac{1}{16}) + (13 \times \frac{1}{8}) = 2\frac{3}{16}$;

$(5 \times \frac{1}{8}) + (9 \times \frac{1}{16}) = 1\frac{3}{16}$.

39. (c) DRONGO (bird). The others are:

(a) CLOISTER

(b) COLISEUM

(d) AQUARIUM

(e) BASILICA

(f) ROTUNDA

40. F.

The movement is:

A. 45°

B. 90°

C. 135°

D. 180°

E. 225°

F. 270°

INDEX

(Italics indicate the answer pages)